POCKET IMAGES

Weardale

POCKET IMAGES

Weardale

June Crosby

NONSUCH

First World War victory celebrations at St John's Chapel.

First published 1993
This new pocket edition 2007
Images unchanged from first edition

Nonsuch Publishing Limited
Cirencester Road, Chalford
Stroud, Gloucestershire, GL6 8PE
www.nonsuch-publishing.com

Nonsuch Publishing is an imprint of NPI Media Group

British Library Cataloguing in Publication Data.
A catalogue record for this book is available from the British Library.

ISBN 978-1-84588-433-8

Typesetting and origination by NPI Media Group
Printed in Great Britain

Contents

Introduction

'Twice-cooked cabbage is seldom palatable,' wrote a distinguished scientist many years ago when asked to repeat a highly successful lecture. There is much sense in his remark as repetition sometimes palls, but we hope that this is not the case with the second selection of photographs of Weardale. Within the dale there is a veritable treasure trove of photographic material of considerable interest. Selection was difficult; so many photographs have been generously offered that all could not be included.

A brief historical sketch and an account of the impact of mining, quarrying and farming upon both the natural and built environment of Weardale was given in the first volume so need not be repeated here. This Pennine dale has much in common with the other northern Pennine dales such as Swaledale, Wensleydale and Arkengarthdale: fell scenery, miles of dry-stone walling, sturdy stone buildings, isolated buildings standing out against the skyline, peaty water bubbling over the rocks of burn and beck, the remains of old lead and ironstone workings, humps and bumps on the ground hinting at an ancient past; these are to be found in all the dales. Yet, as well as this commonality, each dale has its own particular character, and of course we all believe that 'our' dale is the best.

Weardale owes much of its character to having been part of the great estates of the bishops of Durham, who used it for hunting, stock rearing, mineral extraction and rent revenue. The dale was remote from the administrative centre of the bishopric at Durham until the road and transport improvements of the eighteenth and nineteenth centuries, and the bishops were away from their diocese more than they were in it so that the dale was controlled by bishops' officers of varying quality and integrity. A long tradition of absentee landlords was established, which on one hand produced a resentment among the often neglected and sometimes abused tenants, and on the other a sturdy independence among a people left to their own devices. The use of the moors as sporting estates in the nineteenth and early twentieth centuries ensured the continuance of absentee landlords and caused ongoing troubles over the right, claimed by long usage, of the Weardale men to take game off the land.

The development of the lead and iron industries and of quarrying provided great employment and encouraged newcomers to settle in the dale, especially during the eighteenth century. (There are still Scottish names in the area and girls called Tamar, indicating their family's origins.) Yet this industrial activity, in the days when employers exercised great power over their workforce, served to create the idea that the dale was exploited by outsiders and that the Church of England was mainly to blame for this neglect and unfair treatment. This belief has been dented only since the Second World War. One has only to read John Lee's book on Weardale to see how, as recently as 1951, to a dalesman born and bred, the Church was still regarded as the 'big bogey' and, with absentee landlords, the author of the area's ills. Mr Lee was echoing similar remarks made by John Graham in his Weardale book of 1939 and Jacob Featherstone's vigorous attack in his book of 1840.

The missionary zeal and compassion of John Wesley and his followers brought not only spiritual awakening, but also hope and self-improvement. The image of the dalesmen as violent, hard drinking and uncivilized gave way to that of a God-fearing community bent on improving themselves, helping each other and showing considerable enterprise in their leisure activities. This regeneration gave to the dale families like the Dawsons, Races and Waltons, who contributed much to the area and, in some cases, to the world 'outside'. It was not until after 1860 that the Church began to actively involve itself in the lives and welfare of the parishioners in the dale. Bishop Pulleine introduced many societies and activities centred on the parish church as did other rectors such as Bishop Ryan. But the old wariness persisted: when the Revd Kilner, rector of Stanhope, endeavoured to revive the virtually extinct weaving industry in the dale as a way of combating the crippling unemployment of the day, his efforts came to naught because his motives were mistrusted.

Lead mining, ironstone working and quarrying had a major impact on the population and upon the landscape of Weardale. The advent of the London Lead Company (often called the Quaker Company) and of the BB Company (Blackett and Beaumont) at the end of the seventeenth and the early eighteenth centuries brought large-scale commercial exploitation of local mineral resources after centuries of small-scale extraction by families such as the Featherstonhaughs. The effect of the decline of those industries from about 1840 was masked by the increase in quarrying activity following the national increase in road and house building. From 1901 the population began to decline, but left the legacy of a surprising number, for a rural area, of larger-sized settlements: Wolsingham, Stanhope and St John's could claim to be towns rather than villages, and then there are Frosterley, Eastgate, Westgate, Daddry Shield, Ireshopeburn, Wearhead, Cowshill and Rookhope.

The traditional industries of quarrying and mineral extraction continue in the dale, as does the type of industry introduced by Charles Attwood's steelworks, but on a greatly reduced scale. What lead ore remains is at such a depth that the working of it is economically impractical under present market conditions. Ironstone has been worked out and there is little accessible fluorspar. Likewise farming, the dale's other staple industry, is nothing like as intensive as formerly. No longer, for example, is there arable farming around Cowshill as there was when the size of the population and its comparative isolation made such farming worthwhile.

All around are the visible remains of past activity: terracing and strips in ancient fields, derelict miner's cottages, the remains of old smelt mills, lime kilns and mines, empty quarries—now the home of the oystercatcher and the merlin. They are a great source of interest for both local people and visitors, but also sad reminders of opportunities for earning a livelihood which have been lost.

New industries or the revival of the old are needed for the dale if a balanced and continuing community is to be maintained. Young people need to be offered the opportunity of staying here. At present the dale population is an ageing one, as is the population nationally, but our average age is higher than the national average, though not yet as high as Bournemouth which has been nicknamed 'Costa Geriatrica'. There are a few signs of hope: Blair's factory, established at Stanhope after the last war, is continuing under new management and may expand; the Eastgate Blue Circle cement works, opened in the 1960s, is still working; industrial estates have been established at Wolsingham, Stanhope and Frosterley, though with uneven results. For each unit in use, such as the Hathaway garage at Wolsingham, there appears to be one standing empty. 'Bed and breakfast' is providing diversification for farmers and for those with larger houses; there is a pony-trekking centre and an outdoor centre. The Dales Centre at Stanhope is certainly acting as a honeypot for visitors and is trying to build up business skills among the unemployed. Finally, there is still the dale, with its varied scenery, its long vistas, the delights of the changing season, its rich architectural and industrial heritage, its varied flora and fauna, and above all its quiet and its peace. It is still possible to get away from it all here.

For many, economic salvation lies in exploiting and developing tourist attractions. Others view this with alarm, fearful that that which makes the dale so attractive will be destroyed. The experience of other tourist-orientated areas in the country is quoted: of villages with the majority of houses standing empty for several months of the year, where shops are only open in the summer, where the caravan population outnumbers the resident one, where the former peace of the area is disturbed by the sound of trail-rider bikes, where flora and fauna have been eroded, and where farming and moorland management are rendered almost impossible by the intrusion of people and machines.

Councillors and Planners of Wear Valley District Council have the responsibility of planning the future of the dale. Their new Local District Plan will be finalized in 1993, and it will be extremely difficult for them to achieve the fine balance needed to retain all that which gives the dale its special character and at the same time allow for economic recovery. Even the resumption of the old staple industries would produce problems: the mining, extraction and processing industries brought health hazards totally unacceptable by the standards of the late twentieth century. The memory of past pollution, environmental damage and debilitating diseases makes people understandably wary.

Change is inevitable, for what does not change stagnates and no one would wish that upon the dale. One just hopes that the essential character of the dale can be preserved; that both resident and visitor will be able to enjoy a peaceful walk along the old drovers' road past the Elephant trees; sit in solitude beside the linns, or enjoy a walk across the fells when they are purple with heather and listen to the curlew. But we are all conscious that change can be both swift and destructive, which possibly explains why old photographs which recapture the past are so popular. Perhaps as well as preserving old photographs we should be busily making a detailed photographic record of our present—tomorrow's past.

One

Up-Bye

The Head of Wear, Wearhead

Fed by numerous tiny streams and springs from the heart of the high Pennines, the Killhope and Wellhope Burns unite at Killhopeburn Shield to become the North Grain, whence they flow for about 2 miles before joining with Burnhope to form the River Wear. The hamlet of Wearhead (1,100 ft above sea level) grew up around the meeting of the waters and this view encapsulates the essence of Weardale: water, a cluster of sturdy stone buildings, dry-stone walling, trees on the lower slopes and, rising above, the treeless fells that enclose the dale. Although part of the High Forest of Weardale, areas of Killhope and Wellhope were rented out for summer grazing (shielings) and by the early fourteenth century permanent settlements such as Wearhead, Low Allers and Heathery Cleugh had been established.

The sharp turn at Ireshopeburn leading up to Lanehead, c. 1920. The imposing block on the corner is Midlothian House when William (Willie) Pentland lived there. (The ornamental trees have since gone.) Adjoining is the shop owned by Mr Philipson, a highly competent photographer; some of his work is on display at the Weardale Museum at High House chapel. To the left of the picture, at the side of Midlothian House, is the former post office and grocery shop which was run by Joseph Harrison in the 1890s and by Miss Jennie Pentland in the 1920s. Robert Hodgson is standing outside his grocery and drapers shop with his assistant (possibly his son). The children standing against the wall near the shop are Alice and Winnie Neen, whose father was the policeman in Ireshopeburn.

Ireshope Burn from East

Ireshopeburn, looking westwards, c. 1915. In the left foreground is a wooden snow plough ready for fierce winter weather. The house beyond it, with a window in the gable end, is still there. On the other side of the road, with its sign over the door, is Dawson's shop, behind which were the buildings connected with his farming, butchering and carriers business. Thomas Dawson was running the business during the 1890s; by 1925 William Dawson was in charge. Beyond Dawson's was a general dealers and meal store run by George Temperley during the inter-war years.

Lane Hill, leading up to Burnhope Reservoir via the Causeway road over Dollison's Bridge, the parapet of which is in the left foreground. The bridge carries the narrow road over the Peat Cleugh Sike and passes Ling Riggs (seen in the distance, left). Lonnens off the Causeway road lead to isolated farms such as Wham, Middle Rigg, High Rigg and Slack House. The attractive stone building in the foreground (formerly a Congregational chapel) is now a house. As their names suggest, the Riggs are on ridges of land; Wham, on the other hand, derives from a word meaning hollow or depression. Sike is a tiny stream or sometimes a ditch.

Mr J. Dawson and family outside his shop and home at St John's Chapel. The sturdy stone building, the stone slab roof and sash windows are typical of many buildings in Weardale built or extensively altered in the second half of the nineteenth century. They retain the attraction of the local vernacular while adding the refinements of larger windows and higher ceilings drawn from 'polite' architecture.

The dale under snow has a special beauty of its own as this view, looking towards Copt hill with Burtree in the distance, indicates. Yet the beauty of such scenes cannot compensate for the heartbreak and loss which 'old-style' winters could bring to the hill farmers. While many dream of a white Christmas or good sledging or skiing conditions, there are people in the dale who remember the havoc such weather can inflict. In the winter of 1947, for example, all outdoor labour apart from attempts to open the roads was suspended for seven weeks. Hundreds of sheep were lost, many so clogged with ice and frozen snow that they were unable to move and some even had their eyes pecked out by starving birds. No wonder hill farmers are relieved that the Dickensian winters seem to be a thing of the past. Yet the weather can still 'show its teeth' with cold wet weather during lambing time and unseasonal snow (in June 1993 the top of the dale was a white world for two days).

WEEDS.   WESTGATE.

Weeds, a delightful Weardale farmhouse on the north-east side of Westgate, is little changed outwardly from the drawing of 'Weeds, near Westgate' by Jacob John Featherston published in his *Weardale Men and Manners* 153 years ago. It stands just west of the boundary of Stanhope Park and so was within the High Forest of Weardale. Its original name was New Close and it was one of the many farms carved out of the old forest area by the Bishop of Durham's agents in the early fourteenth century. With farms such as Shallowford, Pinfold House and Hanging Wells it represents the changeover from the hunting park economy to stock farming. Stanhope Park was retained as a deer park, its 7 square miles a mere fraction of the 60 square miles set aside for hunting in the twelfth century. The Hodgson family held Weeds for many years; Joseph was farming there at the end of the last century and the family were still there in the late 1920s.

A group posed outside the King's Head Inn, St John's Chapel, admiring the fine Clyno motor car which belonged to Dr Wrench, who is in the group wearing a bowler hat. The notice 'Stable and Motor Accommodation' over the entrance to the inn yard is an indication of changing times: the car is beginning to challenge the horse.

The secluded and substantial High Mill at Westgate stands on the Middlehope Burn. Its garden makes an attractive approach to Slit Wood, one of the loveliest places in the dale. Traces of the mill race are clearly visible and one has only to see the burn in spate to appreciate the driving power of water. It is difficult to imagine that millions of years ago there was a clear sea and coral reef here, and that over countless years the reef was smothered by thick mud, thus gradually forming the Scar limestone and making possible one of Weardale's staple industries. In the wood there are many indications of the considerable mining operations that were here in the late eighteenth and in the nineteenth centuries.

A panoramic view of Rookhope including Boltsburn, which 'looks as if it had been dropped down amongst the hills', wrote Herbert Smith in 1887. The white front of the Rookhope Inn, with its inn sign, stands out clearly. At the extreme left is the village school, erected in 1875 and still in use. In the centre background is Hylton Terrace, nicknamed Blue Row locally. The Rookhope burn, with a low footbridge across it, is at the extreme right. The unfinished building is the mine manager's house. The Rookhope to Middlehope and Rookhope to Parkhead mineral railway used to run through the village. At the top left is Railway Cottages, built to house the men working on the railway; both homes and line have gone. There were several leadmines, a dressing plant, a smelt mill and quarries. It would be difficult to remember this in the quiet village if it were not for the considerable remains of its industrial past. There is currently under discussion a scheme to restore some of the surviving buildings and machinery so that visitors may appreciate the former industrial importance of the area.

Wolf's Cleugh, c. 1900. A rear view of the now derelict cottages which once housed several mining families. The houses were set into the bank, a once common practice in the dale, which must have made the houses very damp. The meaning and pronunciation of 'Cleugh' puzzles many visitors. It means a steep-sided valley or ravine and is a common element in local names, as in Peat Cleugh Sike and Black Cleugh. Its use appears to be confined to northern upland England, though it is listed in the *Shorter Oxford Dictionary* and so is not a dialect word. In Scotland the word occurs as 'cleuch', as in Buccleuch. Locally it is pronounced 'cluff'.

A photographic postcard marked 'near Westgate'. It is a view taken from the south bank of the river looking roughly north-west. In the right foreground is Britton's Hall, in the distance is Sidehead.

Waterside, near Westgate, was once three cottages, one with a stable beneath. It is now one, the home of Mr and Mrs Frank Walton. One of the cottages was occupied in the 1920s and '30s by Miss Jessie Patterson, whose pleasant watercolours enhanced John Lee's book about Weardale. The wooden railings, the stone roof, the cherry tree and the apple tree on the wall have gone, but the sturdy stone house survives. Mr Walton remembers picking apples from the bottom window when a boy; he thinks that the little lad in his Sunday best set off with lace collar is his uncle John Willis.

A charming sketch by William Haitlie, 1887, of one of the Misses Hildyard walking outside Horsley Hall, the family's summer home and shooting lodge near Eastgate. Horsley Hall is a seventeenth-century house with eighteenth- and nineteenth-century additions. J.R. Hildyard commissioned architect Anthony Salvin to extend the house and refurbish the old part around 1850. This Salvin did most successfully, giving it a pleasant and uniform façade. The building was extensively renovated around 1976 after being used for farming purposes (some can remember straw being stored there and hens running in and out).

Cragside farm, Eastgate, seen from the rear, *c.* 1900. It has been the home of the Ward family for over a century. The original farm was one of the ten new farms created in the early fifteenth century by the bishopric officers, though it had been used previously for summer grazing, as its old name, Estyatshiel, indicates. It has been suggested that this was the bailiff's house mentioned in the *Rookhope Ryde*, a ballad of 1572 recording a raid on Weardale by Tynedale robbers:

> Then word came to the Bailiff's house,
> At the east-gate, where he did dwell;
> He was walked out to the Smae-burn,
> Which stands above the Hanging Well.

Two

Stanhope

This pre-1914 view of Stanhope Moor was taken at high summer above the top of Stanhope Dene. Although the growing season in the Pennine dales is short—only four months compared with, say, Devon's seven—growth rate is fast and many visitors are surprised by the luxuriant foliage of a Weardale summer. Trees survive in unlikely places, even if their shape is contorted by the wind. Their worst enemy on the moors are the grazing sheep who do not give young seedlings a chance to mature.

An evocative picture of Stanhope Front Street, c. 1890, when the main road was still a 'dirt road'. The three-storey building, which still survives, was the home of the Fenwick family in the mid-nineteenth century, but was later subdivided. Rowells, the present hardware shop (once Jossie Bee's watch repairers shop), has the original doorway. The buildings with the steep stone roofs have been replaced by Limetree House and the Midland Bank. Beyond the three-storey building is the path alongside the newsagents. When the Methodist chapel was in High Street it was used as a short cut by people going to services.

Front Street, Stanhope, during an 'old-style' winter, c. 1920. The tree overhanging the road at the left is part of that vanished row. At the right of the picture 'Barber' Golighty's pole proclaims his occupation. For about forty years John Golightly and his son John William were the local barbers and for part of that time were newsagents as well. Beyond Golightly's is the post office before the late Mr Henderson altered it. The building near the lamp-post, now Castleside Butchers, was the Bon Café, run for many years by Mrs Elizabeth Fleming and her family.

A view across Stanhope from the south, looking towards Crawleyside and Stanhope Common beyond, around 1875. Field barns are the only buildings on the fields in the foreground now covered by the Bond Isle estate. Beyond the village East Lane, or Gilligate, rises steeply towards the moors. Jolly Body farm stands out to the east of the lane; it was carved from the fell and the Bond Field of the open-field system. On one old document the farm is called Holy Body, and one of its fields the Easter Field. Dales Terrace (which took its name from the strips or 'doles' of the ancient field system) had not been built when this photograph was taken, so the façade of the 1858 Workhouse is seen as its architect Matthew Thompson intended—an imposing 'pauper palace' designed to impress the passer-by. In this early photograph the great Ashes Quarry has not yet slashed its way across Crawleyside to East Lane and beyond. At the top left the beginnings of quarrying and the remains of the old Grove Rakes workings can be seen.

Cowgarth Hill by William Heatlie, 1887. Although cameras had been used in the dale for over thirty years by the time William Heatlie made this careful sketch, no photograph of this spot has been found. The thatch-roofed cottage shows clearly the steep pitch of such roofs, designed to throw off winter rain and snow. The house beyond the thatched cottage survives, as does the footprint of the old cottages although they have been demolished or altered beyond recognition.

Cowgarth Green, Stanhope, c. 1915. The stone steps lead up to the joiner's workshop of Robert Alsopp Turnbull and, later, of Walter Turnbull senior. The ground floor was a house, and in Walter Turnbull's time became Bob Brown's fish shop. Several houses in Stanhope had outside staircases added to them during the nineteenth century; it was a convenient way of dividing them when there was a housing shortage. Most of such staircases have been removed; this one was demolished around 1960. It is thought that the only outside steps surviving in the village are the ones alongside the shop at the corner of Union Lane. The shop with the man and child standing outside was Clyde Raine's in 1914. At the extreme right is the gatepost of the Primitive Methodist chapel and schoolroom. Though the building line remains the same, a comparison between this picture and the 1887 drawing by Heatlie suggests that there had been much rebuilding.

A view of Bridge Street, Stanhope, looking towards West End, with Paragon House on the edge of Cowgarth Green in the distance. The site of the 'new' Town Hall, erected in 1901, can be seen on the middle right and beyond it Wayside, now the home of Mr and Mrs A. Pratt but then the offices of Hodgson's the solicitors and previously a meal store. Beyond Wayside is the police station of 1858. The houses in the foreground, which were older than their Georgian-style windows suggest, have all gone. They were built of local coursed rubble, had heavy stone roof slabs and to enter them one stepped down into the front rooms. On the left is the long wall, encircling the castle grounds.

This photograph nearly continues from the previous one. The shop with the bay window above was the Garnet Café where many people in Stanhope remember buying sweets before the excitement of their weekly visit to the cinema show in the Town Hall. Behind the shop were some small almshouses. The two pedestrians are walking past Joseph Ridley's drapery shop. Mr Ridley used to collect laundry on an old 'sit up and beg' bicycle with a large basket on the front. The scene is now much changed; the line of the road has been modified and the buildings in the foreground demolished. Modern buildings, flats and a fire station now occupy the area.

Although Stanhope Market Place has been much photographed over the years, this view is a little unusual as it shows (left foreground) the *rear* of the shop which jutted out into the Market Place until it was demolished in 1934. The house and shop were successively occupied by the shopkeeping families of Fenwick (1890s), Snowball (c. 1914), and Daley (1920s). The garden must have been triangular in shape as there was, and still is, a 'cut' or path down to Butts Head from Front Street. Stanhope Hotel is now Fisher's electrical and fashion shop. Matthew Curry was the publican in 1902; he was followed by the Gowton family who kept it for about twenty years. Beyond is the former Red Lion Inn and Red Lodge, now private homes though one offers 'B&B' for visitors. The façades of these two buildings were painted red, which presumably explains the names. Some Stanhope residents can remember the paint being removed.

A glimpse of old Stanhope: Leonard Atkinson at the door of his grocers shop, *c.* 1902. The substantial stone building with the local stone roof tiles and monolithic doorway is a good example of Weardale vernacular. It is an old building currently being restored; internal inspection suggests a date around 1670. Like many old buildings it has been altered and renovated (the photo shows four different window types: the Yorkshire sliding sash, the sixteen-pane Georgian sash, the four-pane Victorian and, of course, the shop window inserted into the house front). The closed door is a later addition, giving separate access to the family living quarters. This building was for many years the home of George Morgan, a popular local artist whose work was exhibited at the Society of Northern Artist's exhibitions in Newcastle. The passageway alongside the building remains and leads to the only survivor (now owned by Mr and Mrs I. Richardson) of former almshouses.

A view of the famous Stanhope lime trees in Front Street taken from near the Queen's Head in the early 1930s. On the left is Hartwell School, with charming round-headed windows and shutters since removed. The school, with house, stable and garth for the schoolmaster, was bequeathed to the village by the Revd William Hartwell, Rector of Stanhope 1685–1725, but was closed in 1890; it was used for many years by the County School for woodwork and cookery classes. On the right is the former Weardale Savings Bank premises (c. 1870) which also housed the Mechanics Institute. The distinctive pattern on the roof is very reminiscent of S.S. Teulon's work at Hunstanworth. For some years it was a branch of the Trustee Savings Bank. Since 1988 the building has stood empty awaiting transformation to a restaurant.

The falls above Widley Bridge, Stanhope Dene, c. 1910, '… a scene of charming variety of wood, rock and stream … recently brought to its present state of perfection' (an 1894 guide book). Although an area of considerable industrial activity—mining, smelting, quarrying—the Dene has managed to retain its undoubted beauty and maintain a great variety of plants, especially ferns. In 1892 striking quarry workers repaid the kindness of those helping their families by giving their time and skills to improve the Dene. Sadly their rustic summerhouse has gone, the paths they cut have deteriorated and only the base of their bandstand survives. But that 'state of perfection' of 1894 may in part return. The Weardale Society, with the co-operation of the Church Commissioners and their tenants, is currently organizing improvements.

Many people enjoy visiting old churches as they find them 'peaceful and unchanging' (church visitor's book). Peaceful they certainly are and the calm quiet which meets the visitor to well-cared-for churches such as High House chapel and St Thomas' is something to be treasured in this rackety world. But churches and chapels are not frozen in time. They are changed and adapted to suit the needs and ideas of the people who worship in them. Two photographs of 800-year-old St Thomas', taken about thirty years apart, illustrate this point. This photograph was taken after the alterations of 1867 when the oak pulpit, the seventeenth-century chancel screen and reredos, the oak pews with pineapple finials, the red and black texts on the walls and the harp that stood in the chancel were removed.

In this post-1920 picture of the church decorated for Easter, a brass eagle lectern has replaced the stone pulpit and a new oak pulpit has been placed on the north side of the chancel. The hanging lights have gone. The insertion of the chancel screen has markedly altered the view down the church by making a clear demarcation between chancel and nave. Peaceful, yes, unchanging, no.

The vanished Primitive Methodist chapel in The Square. The Primitive Methodists were active in Stanhope from 1821. At first, regular meetings were held outside St Thomas' church, but later in nearby houses. The chapel was built in 1849, but extensive alterations in 1873 and 1876 made a virtually new chapel. Its demolition was a loss to the area's architectural heritage for it was in a style quite different from any other church in the dale. It had a high barrel-vaulted ceiling and elaborate plasterwork, fine ironwork, and overall was a dignified building. The schoolroom and other buildings are being converted to housing after serving as a clothing factory from 1964.

A view of Stanhope from the West End in 1853, with the Queen's Head on the right. The turret of the castle can be seen in the distance. The land in the left foreground is now modern housing. This washed drawing was made by William Gray, secretary to the Yorks Railway Company. William and his brother Samuel had been tutored by the Revd Mr Goldsmith of the Curatage, Stanhope, in the 1820s. William took advantage of the railway extension to Frosterley to visit old haunts; he wrote a letter about his visit and sent it, with this drawing and three others, to his brother who was a clergyman working in South Africa.

Three

Down-Bye

Harehope Quarry, on the eastern outskirts of Frosterley—an impressive illustration of the massive physical impact of such workings upon the landscape. It is no longer worked, yet once it was the major source of Frosterley marble which is found in many churches of the north-east, including Durham Cathedral. Much regretted by local people was the loss of the fine avenue of trees leading up to Broadwood, which was destroyed by quarrying. It is pleasing to report that the quarry owners, the Council and a local farmer are co-operating to replace lost trees and to remove the debris of industrial activity.

Rogerley Hall, Frosterley (demolished c. 1953), from the south. Outwardly the building seemed of a seventeenth-century date; mention is made of curious oak carvings and of oak panelling. One writer records that there were two old walls in the house 5 ft thick, suggesting a defensible building around which the house developed. Sir Lionel Maddison was the owner in the seventeenth century; highly influential in the Newcastle coal trade his estates passed by marriage first to the Vanes and then to the Londonderry family of Wynyard. Cuthbert Rippon, MP, purchased the property in 1822 and there were Rippons at Rogerley for over a hundred years.

The first service in the new church of St Michael and All Angels was held on 27 May 1869 with Charles Baring, Bishop of Durham, and the first vicar J.H. Scott officiating. The architect was George E. Street. During the next thirty years much was done to improve the fittings. Three new bells were hung in 1878; made by Mears and Stainbank. A Wainwright organ was installed in 1883. Miss Rippon presented the reredos in 1899. Although the 'home' of Frosterley marble, Frosterley had the only church in the dale without some Frosterley marble in it. Thanks to the initiative of Mr Basil Noble and much energetic fund-raising in the village, Frosterley church had a refurbished Frosterley marble font installed three years ago.

William Heatlie's 'facile pencil' (to quote Revd Hoopell) drew this row of houses on the north side of Frosterley in Front Street. The present Frosterley House is against the trees in the background. The cottages are still there, though the tiny paned windows and their hood mouldings have gone.

Two public houses side by side in Front Street, Frosterley, though its proper name is the Lobley Hill Road. Behind the trees is Frosterley House. It is difficult to imagine that the horse, waiting patiently for its rider, is standing roughly on the spot where, about fifty years later, Mr Stan Robinson (see p. 59) was busily at work.

A lovely bird's eye view of Bridge End, Frosterley, with the Primitive chapel and Bridge End Cottage nestling against the burn, the school beyond, and then the climb to Whelpshill End, now just called Hill End.

Front Street, Wolsingham, c. 1920. The two shops with dormer windows and mock half-timbering are immediately recognizable today as George White's, a well-known estate agent, and Second Elegance, whose wares have been praised in the Observer. The Wolsingham Drug Store, prominent at the right, has gone and was replaced by a branch of Martin's Bank and the Bank of Liverpool. It is now a branch of Barclays. The rare chemist's sign—the mortar and pestle—moved along the street to the pharmacy, now run by Mr and Mrs Holden.

Angate Street, Wolsingham. 10242

Angate Street leads up to Upper Town, Wolsingham, and thence up Redgate Bank. The street leaves the Market Place near the former King's Head and turns sharply up the hill, crossing the bridge over the Waskerley Beck. The derivation of Angate is uncertain. It possibly comes from 'an', meaning lonely, and 'gata', meaning street or road. However, it is possible that the first element is from 'angr', meaning grazing land. As descriptive names either could be correct. Though many houses in Angate Street are mid- or late Victorian, there are indications that some are much older and it may well be that some Victorian façades mask much older buildings. In late Victorian times there were several shops in Angate Street, including Miss Pybourne's millinery and drapery store, Thomas Coulson, butcher, George Fleming, boot and shoe dealer, Grundon's the tailor, Robert Hart, Charles Lonsdale, both fruiterers, Robson's, cattle food and drug dealer, Pybourne's forge (p. 51), John Stobbs, butcher, and Mrs Ann Tennick, provision dealer.

There is a pleasant custom in Weardale of giving personal names to places. At Stanhope there is Daniel's Pool and Jake's Falls; at Frosterley there is Kenneth's Bridge; here at Wolsingham there is Jack Walker's Bridge across the Waskerley Beck.

The falls at Wolsingham. Here, as in the preceding photograph, the beautiful setting is being enjoyed by people around the time of the First World War. Luckily both places, like many others in the dale, are still there to be enjoyed by those who love the countryside. Long may they remain so.

St Mary and St Stephen, Wolsingham, in festive mood, date unknown but pre-Second World War. Of the early church only the twelfth-century tower and a re-used door remains. Nave, aisles and chancel were rebuilt (1848–9) in Early English style by William Nicholson, a local builder/ architect. In the churchyard there are several good memorial stones, but one has a particular fascination for visitors—the tomb of sad Jane Garthwaite who cut the throats of two of her children and then her own in 1718. It is recorded that children at the beginning of this century still believed that if they threw flowers on the grave and then knelt down they could hear the children screaming. Somewhat surprisingly, an eleven year old recently assured me that he had done this and it worked—he had heard the screams! Such is the persistence of legend.

Cross House (c. 1895) jutted out across the road at Wolsingham Market Place. As it made the road too narrow for the increasing number of horse-drawn wagons carrying stone from the quarries, it was demolished just before the First World War.

A meticulous drawing by Miss Mary Keenleyside's father, showing the east front of his home, Bradley Hall, 1912. 'Bradeleia' is first mentioned in 1183 and the house has been associated with several important families, including the Eures of Witton, the Tempests (who had their estate forfeited to the Crown for their part in the Rising of the North, 1569), the Bowes of Streatlam, and the Strakers. The line of the medieval moat is practically intact. In about 1820 the house was to be completely refurbished and the sixteenth- and seventeenth-century remains (seen left) were to be incorporated to make a larger house. This scheme was left incomplete, and from this view of the house it is clear that the roof etc. was to be extended further to create a symmetrical building.

Helm Park, or Elm Park as it was sometimes called, is now a hotel, conveniently situated for those wishing to visit Weardale. Formerly it was an old coaching inn with a smithy conveniently placed on the opposite side of the road. The present building hides traces of a sixteenth-century predecessor. It lies within the parish of Thornley, once part of Wolsingham but created a separate parish in 1848, so it is on the edge of the dale. The Helm Park estate, together with Harperley, was acquired by the Pearsons of Durham and by marriage became the property of the Wilkinsons (who converted the inn to a house around 1840) and the Stobarts. The Wilkinsons were keen agricultural 'improvers' in the mid-nineteenth century and the pleasant parkland scenery on their former lands is evidence of their work.

Four

The Daily Round

An odd photograph perhaps to begin this section, yet appropriate; for the powerful influence of local geology upon the dale's landscape and man's activities cannot be exaggerated. From it came the mining, quarrying and stone-cutting industries. The earliest documentary evidence of stone-cutting is in the 1183 survey of his lands ordered by Bishop Hugh du Puiset; Lambert, the marble mason, held 30 acres, rent free, as long as he was working for the bishop. The marble worked by Lambert was Frosterley marble, not a true marble but a limestone full of coral fossils which can be polished to a high gloss with a pleasing pattern. This is a fairly recent photograph by Mr David Hutchinson, but its subject is 325 million years old.

Looking for fluorspar, Boltsburn, *c.* 1910. Fluorspar was mining waste—in other words, it had no use and so no monetary value—until the 1880s when it began to be used as a flux in industry.

Right: Two workers wearily take their break to eat their 'bait' at St John's Chapel. (The church is in the background.) Two 'old timers' join them, no doubt to chat about the time when they were at work. The workmen are wearing heavy clogs, wooden-soled and tipped with iron.

Below: A group of workers outside the crushing plant at Rogerley. The restoration work at Killhope and the re-creation of that site as 'living history' has been imaginatively carried out. But the effect of such dirty and heavy work upon those involved cannot be re-created; men were prematurely aged by long and arduous hours at such plants.

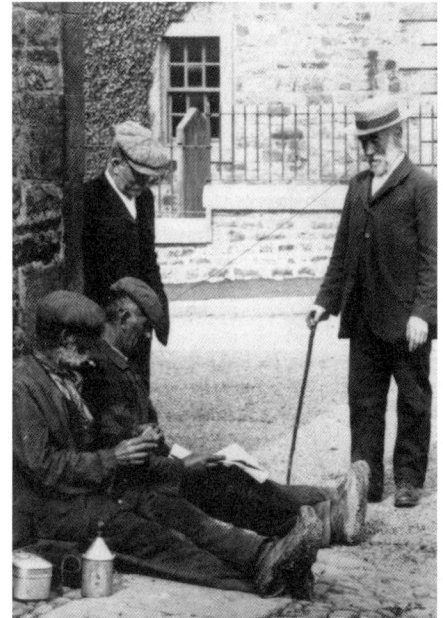

A group of workers outside the Lead Company's offices at Ireshopeburn—all of them with well-known Weardale names. From left to right: Joseph Egglestone, Jack Watson, Isaac V. Philipson, Tom Heatherington (blacksmith), Willie Egglestone, Thomas Edwin Dawson, Matthew Nattress, Ralph Philipson (Isaac's father).

A group of quarrymen posing for their photograph at the quarry face. Although they had the advantage of working above ground, quarry workers had a job about as hazardous as the miners. Accidents often left men disabled and there was considerable risk of lung disease arising from the dust and from the fumes left by blasting. Considerable skill and strength was expected of the quarrymen, yet they were poorly rewarded.

Two kinds of 'workhorse' side by side (for many employers did regard their workforce as such). Face workers at the quarry pose with one of the many draught-horses used in the quarries. Robert Turnbull sits astride the horse, with Clyde Woodhall on his right and Mr Hewitson and then Fred Woodhall on his left. Christopher ? is at the extreme left of the picture.

An aerial view of the Eastgate Cement Works and quarry, 1966. The great pipe snaking down from quarry to plant is clearly visible. The moors stretch far beyond the great gash of the quarry. Among the trees behind the chimney is the remains of a tiny cottage complete with bread oven. The 'Fairy Holes'—one of the many caves and swallow holes occurring in the limestone, have been quarried away like other curiosities such as the Heathery Burn Cave and Bollihope. The Fairy Holes are said to have had stalactites which were removed by a 'gentleman' to be ornaments in his garden.

The Lead Company shops at Ireshopeburn. Left to right are: Joseph Egglestone, Jack Watson (the clerk), Isaac V. Philipson (also an excellent photographer), Tom Heatherington (blacksmith), Willie Egglestone, Thomas Edwin Dawson, Matthew Nattress, Ralph Philipson (Isaac's father).

A small engine used by the Weardale Lead Company in Stanhope Dene. These small engines coped most efficiently in such difficult places.

Stanhope Burn wagonway, *c.* 1920, when it was still working. The railroad was later turned into a road and trucks replaced steam power; this is now the approach road to the head of the Dene.

Above: Many visitors passing the forlorn solitary arch at Rookhope think that it is part of an old railway. In fact it is the sad, small remnant of one of the largest and busiest smelt mills in the dale which provided a livelihood for many local men and their families. This was a favourite area for local boys before demolition. Mr Peter Bowes remembers racing through the tunnel, cycling over the bridge and roasting potatoes over a fire.

Right: Small trucks on a wagonway running through Rookhope. The mineral railway closed in 1923.

The *Portsmouth* engine standing at Eastgate.

Rural roadworks in progress with a steam roller, *c.* 1928.

The Little Grant, a patent steam engine, locally designed and run. The owners offered to lay roads for 1s. 9d. per cubic foot.

![Industrial Wolsingham photograph]

Above: Industrial Wolsingham, c. 1900. This is the rear of one of several industries which flourished in the Causeway area at Wolsingham in the last century. The Causeway was originally the way local farmers drove their cattle to graze on Wolsingham South Moor. The road is now lined by modern housing.

Left: The industrial success achieved at his Wolsingham Steelworks by Charles Attwood was continued by his heir, John Rogerson. Rogerson and Company Ltd acquired an international reputation in the making of ship hulls and anchors for ocean-going liners. Rigorous testing was required before delivery and this illustration shows a test in progress.

DROP TEST FOR ANCHORS.

Opposite: The fine tomato house at Stanhope Rectory, designed to capture maximum light and sun. Tomatoes were a speciality of the gardener Mr Briggs of Hartwell House.

Left: This is part of an old thresher, worked by steam, which once was at a farm 'near Frosterley'.

Below: A solitary yeddle pump, ugly but useful as it pumped up the liquid from the midden to be used for fertilizer on the fields.

The interior of the old blacksmith's forge, Angate Street, Wolsingham, disused but with its tools and anvil remaining *in situ*. The forge was last worked by the Pybourne family; a descendant, Mr W.G. Pybourne, still lives in the town and is a craftsman joiner.

The exterior of the same eighteenth-century forge, with stone slab roof and brick chimney. It was due for demolition in 1970; fortunately it was not lost, but dismantled and taken to be used at Beamish Open Air Museum near Stanley.

This is a somewhat risky inclusion. The Beamish Museum Photographic Archive and an up-dale resident have identified it as Upper Weardale; Bowes Museum as Teesdale. Both agree it is Robert Ferguson. It is such a fascinating shot, showing all the paraphernalia of a trade which was practised in all the larger settlements of Weardale, that it has been included in spite of its doubtful provenance.

Right: The formation of County, Rural and Urban Councils created new job opportunities. After serving in the First World War, Mr Jimmy Ridley of the White House, Stanhope, was able to follow a successful career in local government. He ran the Weardale Rural District Council offices at Fairfield House and took an active part in local activities, including being secretary of the Stanhope Silver Band. His wife was the former Miss Evelyn Mews of Stanhope Old Hall.

Below: Building Co-operative Terrace, Stanhope, now Paragon Street, *c*. 1903.

An 'old father time' of Weardale, Mr J. Hockaday, sharpening his scythe or 'mower'. It took years of experience to achieve the efficient rhythmical swing that was the hallmark of the expert and which allowed him to work for the long hours demanded at hay-making time.

Hay was essential for the success of the farmer and at haymaking time everyone was pressed into service. Here is a group of reapers at the ready with the simple but backaching tools they used. Behind them is a 'pike'; its construction was not as simple as one might think. First a firm outer base of hay was made, then the centre was filled in; this was followed by another circle of hay, a little smaller than the first outer layer, and the centre of this was filled in. The process was repeated, each outer circle being a little smaller than the previous one and so the cone shape was achieved. One worker could make a pike, but if two were available then one of them would stand on the inner pile of hay to tread it down.

Sheep being driven down Front Street, Stanhope, date unknown but probably around 1860. This picture has been published as a photograph in William Morley Eggerstone's *Memorials of Bishop Butler*, and as an engraving, and a copy was painted by the late George Morgan. The original artist is unknown. One thing is certain—no shepherd of today would dare drive his sheep down Front Street. Once in the dale, this road is the only road giving access up the dale and is becoming busier and busier.

Above: Two sisters with their prize-winning rams. The grooming and preparing of stock for showing is still a time-consuming task. Before the introduction of the sheep dip in the 1880s, it must have been very tiresome and smelly. In order to keep them healthy and free from tics before the advent of dipping, sheep were greased. This involved holding the sheep over a stool, parting the hair in sections and rubbing in fat (often rancid butter). Even a skilled man took about 45 minutes to grease just one animal.

Left: To a hill farmer a strong ram is a prized possession; if horns are any indication this young man would seem to have a good blackface. He is not dressed for working so perhaps he has hauled the ram out of the field for the Eastgate or another show.

Taking a break from sheep shearing at Stewart Shield Meadows to circulate the billycan. Standing at the back is Harry Stephenson, a former quarryman, who was present at the uncovering of the fossil trees. The Collingwoods are clustered near the front, the Mews boys are behind. Sheep shearing was a hard but sociable task in pre-mechanization days. The womenfolk took the 'bait' to the workers, neighbours came over to watch, to offer advice, perhaps to help, children often played truant to join in, and there were sing-songs in the evening. Shearing too was a skilled job—a slip of the shears could cause a bad cut which could easily become infected and weaken or kill the animal.

Many visitors to Weardale think of it as an entirely sheep-farming dale, but the pastures along the riverbank are surprisingly rich and well adapted for fattening cattle as well as lambs. The two cows here are fair specimens and their owner from Peakfield is happy enough to have her photograph taken with them, dressed in her Sunday best. There was a Cow Club founded in the dale in the second half of the nineteenth century which survived until the Second World War. In 1937 the annual subscription was 3s.; if a member's beast died he received £11.

Miss Jane Ann Ridley of Peakfield, Frosterley, with a group of contestants at an agricultural show. The role women played on the farms is sometimes overlooked, yet in addition to all the usual chores they were in charge of the poultry and butter and cheese making. At one time butter making was an essential skill for the farmer's wife and Miss Jane Ann Ridley was an expert who achieved a wide reputation and acted as a dairy instructress.

Right: Dora and Hannah Blenkinsop getting to work, *c.* 1910. The wicker clothes basket, the wooden bucket, the poss-stick and tub, and the wash board were their tools, backed by 'elbow grease'. The rectangular tub is for rinsing. One of similar shape was used for dyeing.

Below: A passing motorist, amazed to see a *man* sweeping away water outside the Forrester's Arms, Frosterley, stopped to take a photograph of publican Mr Stan Robinson at work. On the opposite side of the road is the village hall, where Mrs Laura Hartshorne and her co-workers now have a tempting crafts market. Tucked away between it and little Roseli Cottage (at the extreme left) is the former oratory chapel built in 1834 for the villagers by Revd W.N. Darnell, rector of Stanhope.

The days of gracious living—at least for the affluent. Some of the servants at Newton House when it was still the Roddam home: the gardener, the cook, the odd job and poultry man, the upstairs maid, the downstairs maid, and the gardener's boy.

From the washing tub into the mangle (probably at St John's Chapel, *c.* 1930), with young son to help guide the clothes through; the worst job was making sure that breakable buttons were arranged to go over the edge of the rollers and not through them. Washing by hand in the backyard was a cold job except in the hottest of weather.

For many craft workers quilting is now a pleasant pastime. In the nineteenth and early twentieth centuries making a quilt was part of a housewife's work. Young girls made them in readiness for their 'bottom drawer'. Quilting 'parties' were held and so quilt making served a social function as well. The following photographs of skilful lower dale quilter Mrs Lough demonstrate the three main steps in making a quilt. The first step is the drawing out of the design.

The second step is fixing the material on the frame and sewing by hand the thousands of tiny stitches required to produce the pattern.

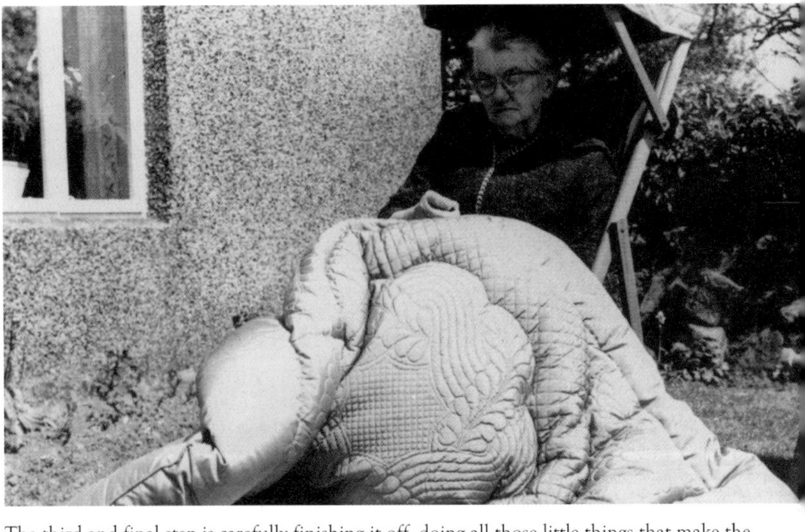

The third and final step is carefully finishing it off, doing all those little things that make the difference between expert and amateur effort.

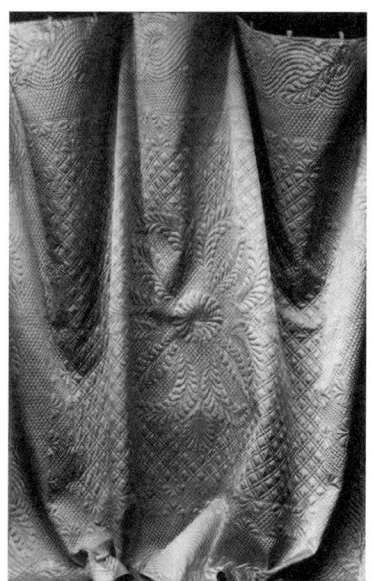

Weardale has a fine tradition in quilting and the craft has had a revival recently. Veteran quilter Mrs Amy Ems had made the Weardale patterns nationally known. Mrs I.J. Wiles of Wolsingham is another highly experienced and respected craftswoman. This is a very special quilt made and designed by her for the Marchioness of Normanby.

The knitters of the Yorkshire Dales, especially around Dent, are well known. The same tradition existed in Weardale though it was not so widely known or publicized. Many women knitted socks for families and sometimes for profit. This is the only photograph found so far of a Weardale knitter. It was taken 'in a field near St John's Chapel'. The woman's white headgear was usual for women working in the fields; the Weardale Museum has a few examples.

Above: During the Second World War the Women's Land Army (only disbanded a few years ago) helped to keep farms going at a time when home-produced food was vital because of the blockade at sea. These are Land Army girls stacking wheat, a hand-wrecking, backaching job.

Left: 'Going for potatoes'—a good period piece, beautifully captured by the camera.

The hardworking Revd Mr Shaddick, this time outside the south porch door of St Thomas' church, surrounded by oh-so-solemn and angelic-looking choirboys in the late 1920s. Where are they now?

This is a rare photograph of the staff of Westgate School in 1908, complete with a 'pupil teacher'. Education opened the door to new opportunities for many young people in the dale, especially for the girls. No longer was domestic service, marriage and family their inevitable lot; a basic education gained them entry to white-collar jobs, including teaching.

The horse is the unsung hero of the dale. Before steam, electricity and the internal combustion engine, workhorses made a major contribution to the economy of the dale—they ploughed, drew heavy loads of stone, carried lead, carried their masters and drew the carriages for the women, so the next few pages are devoted to these hardworking creatures.

This is Mr Tom Currah (left) with his heavy draught-horses at Parson Byers.

Mr Dent on his horse, possibly at Eastgate. Such sturdy animals were ideal for carrying a farmer about his business.

Good breeding stock was essential and Mr Joseph Currah of Parson Byers is justifiably proud of his mare and her foal with a white blaze.

This is a horse-drawn reaper, which was widely used in the dale at one time.

A working horse, an equine 'Jack of all trades', photographed at Eastgate. These sturdily built animals, about 13 ½ hands high, were useful for draught and as a mount. In the early part of this century some farmers began breeding a larger horse of about 15 hands, but many traditionalists thought the old size 'could na' be beat'.

This high-wheeled cart belonged to the Stanhope and Weardale Co-op and was used for delivery. The animal shows the thickset character, broad chest and longish mane of these all-purpose animals developed from the Galloway.

Here horses are being used for gathering potatoes. One man guides the horse and reaps while two pick up the potatoes. For once the collie, another 'workhorse' of the dale, is not having to work.

The mighty Clydesdales at Wolsingham Show. The heavy draught-horses always attract a crowd. Their numbers fell somewhat worryingly after the Second World War, but they are increasing now. There is a revival in their use on the farm, and leading breeders, which include HM The Queen, are increasing stocks.

A pony and trap outside Stanhope Castle. A glitter sticker has been affixed to use the photograph as a Christmas greetings card. The doorway in the background led to the headmaster's house—the castle was used as a boys' school after the Second World War.

A pony and trap outside Parson Byers Farm.

An up-dale farmer forks hay while the horse draws the sled which was used for carrying loose hay.

Winding the pike of hay. The weather is a constant worry at hay-making time, and this was particularly so when it was done by hand. After cutting, the hay was spread over the field to dry. If the outlook was uncertain then the workers would have to pile the hay into 'half rucks'—tiny haycocks—in the hope of protecting it. It often had to be spread out again until dry. This process might have to be repeated before the hay could be made into pikes. The pikes were eased on to the sledge-like cart shown here, winched up and taken to the farmyard.

Mr Issy Thompson with his reaper.

John Betjeman sang the praise of the motor bike and used it in his explorations around the English countryside. The motor bike was an advance on the push-pedal bicycle as it enabled people to travel further and faster. Mr W. Bell is rightly proud of his machine for it gave him great independence in work and leisure. Descendants of these machines are now regarded as standard farm equipment by many landowners.

Horse and steam power side by side: a Weardale Highways Board's water cart. Horses continued to be used alongside cars, tractors, steam engines, etc. for many years. Many farmers could not afford the new machinery and coalmen, milkmen and fruiterers tended to stick to horse and cart as well. As one milkman said, 'a horse will follow you; a van can't.' In the background of this photograph is the bridge that connected Stanhope Castle and the gardens on the other side of the road.

Five

Joys and Pleasures

Assembling for a carnival parade near the Boltsburn mine at Rookhope, c. 1919. Part of the spoil heap can be seen at the right. Rookhope Carnival is still a happy annual event, but it is not certain if this photograph is of the carnival or an extra celebration for the end of the war.

A 'live' game of Bridge on the Rectory lawns, Stanhope. Mrs Nellie Stephenson is the Joker, Miss Hannah Robinson, Crawleyside WI, is on her right. In the front row, from left to right, are: Mary Lonsdale, Ella Bibby, Cilla Elliott, Winnie Tinkler, Doris Waller and Queenie; and Mrs A. Turnbull, organist at St Thomas' church, Stanhope, for over forty years, can supply the names of all the others as well. For she was little Annie Pattinson who was sitting on the chair at the extreme right when this photograph was taken nearly seventy years ago.

The Revd Mr Shaddick, a Stanhope curate, was keenly interested in music and active in encouraging social events. This photograph was taken at a church social which was held in the former Methodist chapel, now Chapel Cottage and No. 5 High Street. Many of the people in the group have been identified. Mrs Shaddick is sitting at her husband's right. At the left end of the front row is Jimmy and Jean Parmley's grandmother, and next door but one is Mrs Maud Pattinson (Mrs Annie Turnbull's mother). Third from the right is Miss Mary Graham who became a deaconess. In the second row at the left with his hand behind his back is Mr Snowball of the Market Place shop; behind him at the back is Tommy Bainbridge, the sexton. Mr McCollum (with moustache) is standing behind the curate, with Maggie Thompson on his right. The 'musical Woodhalls', so closely associated with Stanhope Brass Band, are well represented. Mr Clyde Woodhall (with moustache) is at the left behind the lady with the light-coloured dress; his wife is in the front row, second left; Willie Woodhall is at the right of the photograph behind another lady in a light-coloured dress; and Jack Woodhall is just behind him looking over someone's shoulder.

Opposite below: The Friends of Horn Hall have done consistently wonderful fund-raising for the hospital for many years. Here is one of many such efforts in 1970. From left to right: Rachael ?, Mary March (now of Rookhope), Nurse Agnes Dargue, the stallholder who generously donated her wares, Matron Margaret Slater, the late Dr Donald Thompson and 'Dr Mrs' Betty Thompson. The Thompsons were the doctors in Stanhope for over forty years. Their services during that time are remembered with great affection and respect. Mrs Thompson is still keenly interested in Stanhope affairs.

The High House Wesley Guild (before 1929) photographed at Coronation Bridge corner, with the Wesley Thorn and part of the Crossings House behind, with the gates still in use. At the right is part of the Weardale Museum which opened in 1985. How many of us faced with such a group could remember 52 names 65 years on? Very few, one suspects, but Mrs O. Peart could and as a tribute to her enviable memory we list the names here. Back row, left to right: Norman Dawson, Edwin Hodgson, Esther Annie Robinson, Ethel Turnbull, Blanche Coulthard, Evie Coulthard, Constance Watson, Harry Coulthard, Florrie Craig, Cissie Oliver, Tom Guy Peart, Olive Heatherington, Harry Walker, May Watson, Gabrielle Rutherford. Third row: William F. Dawson, Isaac Philipson, Rita Philipson, Annie May Watson, Annie Maddison, Mary Jane Walton, Dora Heatherington, Maud Watson, Millie Elliott, Mary Hannah Hodgson, Willie Feathersone, Phoebe Watson, Sally Nattress, John Tom Ridley, Lizzie Watson, Jenny Pentland, Arthur Emerson, Hannah Ridley. Second row: May Philipson, Elizabeth Agnes Philipson, Isabel Jane Coulthard, Alice Feathersone, Revd Wilfred Rhodes, Revd Jackson Cotton, Leonard Coulthard, William Watson, Meggie Watson, Annie Mary Nattress. Front row: Nancy Emerson, Jean Watson, Gordon Watson, Jackie Coulthard, Susie Craig, ? Coburn, Wilf Watson, Willie and Bill Stanley.

Although Boltsburn had a Methodist congregation of twelve members by 1791, the chapel was not built until 1812, so presumably house meetings were held until then. The centenary was an occasion to celebrate and this photograph shows the anniversary tea. A new, larger chapel was built in 1863 as membership was increasing; it 'peaked' in the 1870s when there were 125 members and 120 members of the Sunday school. The 1812 chapel was converted to domestic use and is known as Chapel House.

A special 'chapel' tea party at Rookhope. It would be good to know who, when and why.

A Christian Endeavour group at Bridge End, Frosterley. The ladies are showing the fashions of the late 1920s. Jennie Pattinson is in the front row at the right. Behind her, in a jacket with revers, is Florrie Pattinson. Mrs Dodd is in the back row, second from right. Jennie Stephenson is in the second row, at the left, in a dark dress with a jet necklace. Behind her is Mrs Philipson who later kept the post office at Meadowfield. This was the second Primitive Methodist chapel at Frosterley; the first one, built in 1829, became a house when the 'new' one behind the group was opened in 1861. Today the 'new' chapel, having been used as a store by a local farmer, is to be converted into housing.

Amateur dramatics has always been a speciality of the dale and the tradition is flourishing. There are the Harlequins at Wolsingham, the Phoenix Players at Stanhope and Miss Maxine Raine's 'Kids on Sunday' group at Ireshopeburn. This beautifully costumed cast of the *Quaker Girl* 'soon after the war' is thought to have performed at both Stanhope and Wolsingham.

A cheerful and variously dressed group outside Stanhope Castle. Said to be the cast of a play, with Mrs Hilda Hall sitting in the front row. Any further information would be welcomed.

This is the cast of the *Mikado* at Westgate, taken against some impressive scenery near Daisy Villa. The unidentified spectators certainly had a grandstand view. The names of this happy group read like a roll-call of 'old Weardale' families. They include Emmerson—Harry, Percy and his sister Mary who became Mrs Coulthard of Daisy Villa; Race—George and brothers Thomas and Harold and sister Lizzie; Coulthard—Leslie, Hannah, Mary, Myra; Nattress—Annie and Nellie; Walton—Beatrice and Eric (of Waterside); Muschamp—Nancy and Lena; Gowland—Hugh and Mary, Ethel and Nancy; and the families of Moses, Dalton, Kidd and Rowell are also represented.

Opposite below: An upper-dale fancy-dress competition in April 1918. The Red Cross nurse alongside the more usual fairy, clown and geisha girl is a reminder that the war was still in progress. The hall has not been identified. Could it be the former chapel in Upper Town, Westgate?

A performance of *Cinderella* at the Town Hall, Stanhope, 1945—a popular entertainment initiated by Danny Sneddon and his sister at a time when celebrations were in order. Audrey Cattle is at the right, showing a fine pair of legs in tights; next door to her is Mr Bell as a policeman. The Ugly Sister near him, with high 'hair-do' and fan, is Joseph 'Pater' Allinson, a wrestler. The Prince Charming, holding Cinderella's hand, is Audrey Clish. The good fairy behind is Vera Brown whose father, Redvers Brown, is the other Ugly Sister. The three little girls at centre front are Eileen, Cynthia and someone whose name is unknown, who practised their dance routine so frequently and thoroughly at Mrs Jack Woodhall's that she declared they tap-danced her carpet away.

WOLSINGHAM SHOW 678

Left: Late August–September is Agricultural Show time in the dale. St John's Chapel Show is on the last Saturday in August, Wolsingham and Stanhope Shows are on the first and second Saturday of September and, if you wish, there is Eggleston to be enjoyed on the third. All three Weardale shows have a fair attached to them and many of the fair people travel from one show to the next. This old helter-skelter has not been seen for many a year but once it 'visited' all three Weardale shows. In this photograph of Wolsingham, around 1905, it was situated on the Showfield; at Stanhope it used to be just outside St Thomas' church gate.

Below: How many 'grown men' of today would go to a weekly Bible class? Not many one suspects. Yet once they were a regular feature of cities, towns and villages throughout the country, particularly within the Methodist community. This is Wearhead Bible Class, around 1925, with their leader (book in hand). John Ralph Peart, the father of Mr A. Peart of Woodcroft, is in the back row; further names would be welcomed.

This photograph is labelled 'The Show Committee', but which show and when is not known. No sooner is one show over than the hardworking committee members have to begin preparations for the next. When Stanhope Show moved from Castle Park to its present site, Mr Walter Turnbull had to survey the ground and devise a layout for the marquees, arena and stalls; his plan is still in use.

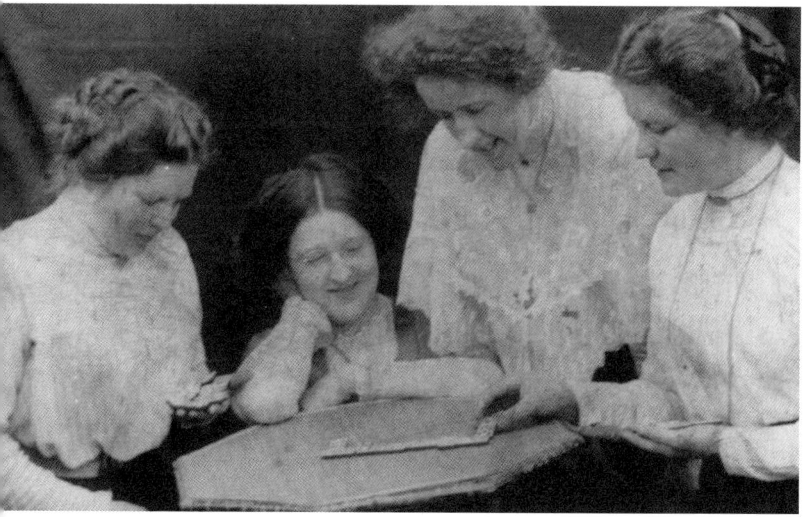

Four ladies, dressed for afternoon tea, concentrate on a game of dominoes around an octagonal bamboo table; such tables were very popular early in the century.

Young Joseph Jackson and Wilf Peart are enjoying the excitement of being close to the Russian 'dancing bear' opposite the Golden Lion, St John's Chapel. The German trainers, their leather wallets across their back, travelled the country exhibiting their bear. It must have been a wearisome life for all three, but one's sympathies are all for the bear with its poor maimed paws. The old-style 'training' in Germany and Poland (now strictly illegal) was horrific. First the bear had its sight impaired; then it was tied to a stake and a white-hot iron passed close to its eyes. To train it to dance the word of command was drilled into the bear by forcing it on to a bed of red-hot charcoal. Naturally the bear stood up trying to avoid the pain. Repeated experience of this pain and the creature would respond to the word associated with the fire by standing on two legs and 'dancing'.

Above: Members of one of the many men's clubs which flourished in the dale. Mr Wilf Lonsdale is in the front row, second from the left.

Right: The 'slide show man' who once delighted audiences at Wolsingham with his lantern shows. His name appears to have been forgotten, but the pleasure the shows gave was considerable, for several people in Wolsingham recall their parents talking about his shows with great affection.

An upper-dale wedding group, c. 1910, a beautiful wedding with gorgeous hats and a delightful little bridesmaid in her picture hat and with long ringlets and posy basket. Wedding outfits were usually 'sensible' at this time, in other words clothes were chosen, even for the bride, with an eye to their future use. The white bridal outfit of bride and bridesmaid and the top hats suggest that this is a wedding in a family that could afford some extra luxuries for such a special occasion. Behind the group, to the right, is Providence Cottage. Next to it is the house built by 'Jock' Robinson, a lead miner who had a lucky strike in Stanhope Burn and built the house, giving it an impressive stone portico that could have graced a mansion. The porch carries the date 1870 and it is said that Mr Robinson built it himself. The photograph was taken in a field now part of the Westgate caravan site.

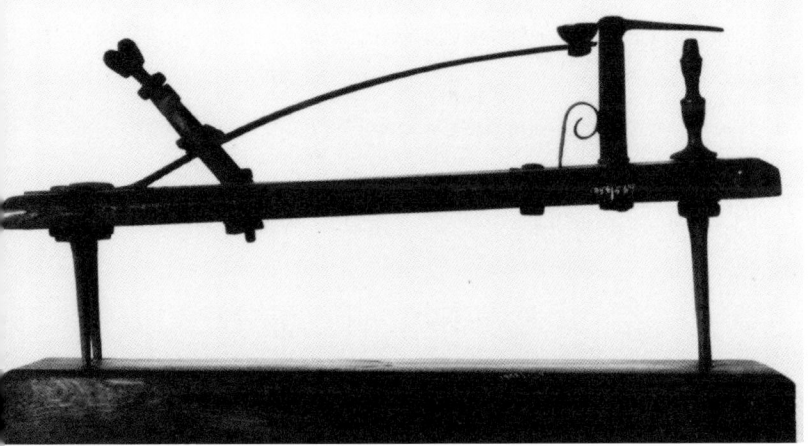

'Holding up the bride' is a Weardale custom described as ancient in 1794. In Stanhope the church gates are locked while the bride and groom are in the church. At Rookhope, where this photograph was taken, the bride is stopped on her way to church.

Knurr and Spell, a now defunct game, was very popular in the north during the eighteenth and nineteenth centuries. Matches were held regularly in the dale, but gradually died out after the First World War. This is the spell, from which the knurr–the wooden ball–was sprung. The Weardale Museum has a wooden spell on show.

Here the player is waiting to hit the knurr with a club whose head is somewhat 'fly-swat' in shape.

Eddie Mason swings his club at the same match. The spectators would appear to have great confidence in the players—they are standing very close in both cases.

The residents of Bond Isle, Stanhope, organized a much needed playground for local children; here they are testing out the equipment around 1950.

Football has been a popular spectator and participation sport in the dale throughout this century. Before the Second World War every village had its own team. This is the Wearhead football team of 1930.

A cartoon by Willie Bainbridge, a Tow Law newsagent, allegedly depicting the consternation caused in Stanhope by the first planes flying overhead. The drawing is dated 1919, the incident on which it is based took place two years earlier. The characters have been identified. Colonel Angus, solicitor, is barking orders at his partner, poor Mr Hodgson, who is falling off his horse. Portly Dr Robinson is flat on his back. The notorious village gossips are so busy talking they are oblivious of the momentous event taking place overhead. The local representative of the 'world's oldest profession' is being taken off to the lock-up by the village policeman.

Music making is a fine and flourishing feature of Weardale life and deserves a special mention. This is the Rookhope Choir about to set off on an engagement around 1929. Most villages had and have their own choirs. Recently the Weardale Singers have been formed in the upper dale to draw singers together and another new group, the Music Makers, is an 'all dale' group.

The Rookhope carollers, complete with squeeze box, triangle and banjo, setting off in the snow for an evening round of calls.

Stanhope Band celebrates the 170th anniversary of its formation in 1993, almost the only survivor. Yet eighty years ago most villages had their own band. The three Woodhalls, Clyde (the father), Jack and Joe, stand in front of Dilly Hill, Stanhope Old Hall. It was the tenacity of first Clyde and then his son Jack which kept Stanhope Band flourishing. Jack Woodhall's daughter, Mrs Ann Harrison, continues a connection with the band, the fifth generation of Woodhall to do so. In 1992 she was mainly responsible for an exhibition on the history of the band held at the Durham Dales Centre.

The old Weardale Band wearing their pillbox hats outside the Cowshill Hotel, when Octavius Monkhouse was proprietor around 1894.

The Stanhope Saxhorn Band announced its 're-establishment' in 1880 and advertised that it would play both sacred and secular music. It delighted dancers up and down the dale for many years. Back row, left to right: Fred Walker, Joe Woodhall, Jack Cleasby, William O'Dell, -?-, Mattie Willis, Redvers Pattinson, Jack Woodhall, Thomas Walton, George Dixon, George Pattinson, Hewitson Dixon. Middle row: Joe Priestman, Jack Nicholson, ? Priestman, Charles Murray (conductor), Leslie Hayton, Jimmy Hayton, John Bowman. Front row: George Cattle, Bob Turnbull, Jack Pattinson, John George Forster, Wilf Brown, Vincent Coatsworth, Leslie Furnace. The band was photographed in 1920.

The Stanhope Band posing in full uniform near the Scout Hut on the Paddocks, Ashes Quarry, 1924. Back row, left to right: Ord Forster, Bill Walton, George Pattinson, Redvers Pattinson, Harold Storey, Dick Calvert, Alfred Jacques. Middle row: John Row (with the drum), Mattie Willis, Joe Woodhall, Jack Cleasby, Harold Raine, Clyde Woodhall, Walter Calvert, John George Forster, Joseph Allinson, George Allinson, Jackie Pattinson, Joseph Wallace, Jack Woodhall, Joe Priestman, Billy Hobson, ? Priestman, George Thompson, and Eric Pattinson at the front. Most of these 'band names' are still in the dale and some of the families still continue the tradition. Douglas Cleasby (great-nephew to Jack in the photo) is conductor of the present band. Young Emily Cleasby is already skilful on the cornet and sister Alice on the drum and flugel; both are enthusiastic members of the junior band.

The Stanhope Band outside Rookhope School, *c.* 1920, with its fine drum which was to be destroyed in a fire about sixty-five years after this photograph was taken. Clyde Woodhall senior is at the extreme left, back row.

The Saxhorn Band, *c.* 1930. Many of the bandsmen were in more than one band and many families such as the Gowlands and Woodhalls are 'band families'.

The Stanhope Band outside the offices of the *Northern Echo*, Darlington, on their way to the 1934 brass band competition in London where they won the silver cup. At the extreme left is Mr Jossie Patterson, an ardent supporter. Another dedicated fan was Mr W. Robinson; he was at the band's last rehearsal before leaving for London and declared that they had played magnificently and that 'if any band beat Stanhope, then that's the band that will win the cup.' He died as he left the rehearsal and so never heard of their success.

A ladies orchestra, charming in graceful white dresses and with Edwardian hairstyles, are pictured with their instruments; the instrument held at the extreme right is a puzzling one.

The Revd Mr Shaddick and his mixed orchestra in the upstairs room of the former Methodist chapel in High Street which became the church hall, the Salvation Army Centre and the Second World War Food Office before being made into two houses. With the curate are Willie Watson at the left, next (inevitably) Clyde Woodhall senior and Willie his brother. At the extreme right is Jack Woodhall, with Charlie Murray next to him. Fred Woodhall has the double bass.

Mr Roger Johnson and his Musical Group were a popular quartet of singers who used to entertain around Wolsingham and further afield during the inter-war years.

Left: The strong music tradition of the dale includes organ music, an essential part of church and chapel services. Mr W.F. Dawson is seated at the J.R. Vincent (Sunderland) organ of High House chapel, Ireshopeburn, which came from the demolished Victoria Hall in Sunderland. Professor Robert Milburn is 'the Mr Dawson of today' and there are happy signs that the tradition will continue in the future. For example, Nicholas Forbes, recently off to Cambridge, is a skilled musician and a composer, whose Mass was given its very first performance in the dale in 1993. The Vincent organ factory also continues; its present owner, Mr Nicholson, is an accomplished organist who has performed on the High House organ.

Below: The Phoenix Inn, now the Bonny Moor Hen, decorated for the coronation of Edward VII which was delayed for a year as he had appendicitis—then a 'new' condition. The date originally fixed for the coronation had to be changed.

The coronation of King George V and Queen Mary in 1911 was celebrated with great enthusiasm and loyalty throughout the country. Stanhope was no exception. This photograph shows the formal part of the celebrations. Soldiers and civilians gathered in the Market Place to hear the official proclamation and speeches by local worthies. The ladies in the foreground show the backs of their costumes for our appreciation. Gently flowing skirts, hip-length flared jackets with nipped-in waists, and wide-brimmed hats make for grace and dignity. The churchyard wall is still unpierced (no War Memorial or fossil tree in 1911), as is the wall of the ornamental and kitchen gardens of Stanhope Castle.

The children's celebrations at Westgate in 1911. Such big parties appear to be a thing of the past. Some readers will remember the street parties and the firework displays that followed the end of the Second World War.

Westgate coronation parade, 22 June 1911–a group of ingenious costumes and a clutch of wonderfully decorated bicycles.

Another part of the elaborate celebrations in honour of King George V's coronation in 1911. The horse-drawn procession is passing the main shop of the Weardale and Stanhope Co-operative Society, a building now being extensively renovated by new owners.

The wedding of the daughter of Revd J.J. Pulleine, Bishop of Richmond, a very grand affair with a goodly crowd of sightseers. The church gate was draped and the path covered by an awning for fear the weather would be inclement on the big day. Guests arrived by coach. It must have been *the* social event in Stanhope in 1912.

Freemasons' processions such as this are now extremely rare and can only be held by permission of the Grand Master. This procession through Rookhope, with the masons in their regalia of apron and collar, took place on 30 July 1904 to mark the laying of the cornerstone of the new St John's church, whose incumbent, the Revd Mr Joseph Baker (vicar 1902–13), was an active freemason. The village was *en fête* with banners flying and everyone dressed up in their best. One wonders how long the children will remain so beautifully clean; they look as if they had just stepped out of an E. Nesbitt story.

The last Florence Nightingale Procession was held on a cold wet day in 1974. Eric Robson plays the drum, wearing the Stanhope Band's then new uniform. Rachael Phillips holds an umbrella to protect Matron Margaret Slater, now well known as leader of the Frosterley art group. Behind is Agnes Dargue and Joan Tait. Millie Dixon is the tall lass behind Agnes. Nancy Bowman of Hill End is towards the back, holding her umbrella in a gloved hand.

Crawleyside WI celebrating its third birthday in 1925. They can all be named. Back row, left to right: Gladys Porter, Bessie Raw, Susie Forster, Miss Mawson, Blanche Robson, Mrs Coates, Miss Mawson, Mrs Toombs. Fourth row: Ruth Littlefair, Miss Jordan, Grace Elliott, Jane Pinder, Maude Pattinson, Elsie Angus, Nellie Angus, Violet Sanderson, Mrs Shebbeare, the rector's wife, Nellie Stephenson. Middle row: Miss Philipson, Mary Craig, Bessie Brown, Mrs Heathington, Mrs Muschamp, Mabel Wallace, Mrs Ayton, Mrs Bibby, Mrs Blenkinson, Mrs Emerson, Mrs V. Cleasby, Mrs Osborne. Second row: Miss Philipson, Mrs Coates, Mary Graham, Mrs Harper, Hilda Whitfield, Miss Philipson, Mrs Lonsdale, Mrs Beeston. Front row: Mrs Cattle, Ray Cattle, Miss Earl, Mrs Priestman, holding Freda, Mrs Tinkler, with Harry, Gladys Elliott, Mrs Walker, Miss C. Galley, Mrs Maggie Gray, Mrs Littlefair, with Ronnie, and Mrs T. Elliott, with Sadie who became Mrs Cridge.

The train and then the omnibus opened up the dale to the 'outside'. The railway reached Frosterley in 1847, but did not get to Wearhead until 1895. Then, just sixty-eight years later, the line from Wearhead to Eastgate was closed. This is an event still well remembered, for many schoolchildren and workers travelled down the line every morning. Mr O. Gibson began the first omnibus service in the dale in 1923, with the service from Stanhope to Cowshill beginning in 1925. Its 'descendant', Weardale Motor Services, with Mr Roland Gibson in charge, is still serving the dale–fortunately for us all.

Left: A photograph from Wolsingham recording an obviously important occasion around the time of the First World War. A three-tier iced cake and a proggy mat has been taken outside into the garden, and the lady has lace at her neck and wrists. Perhaps someone could identify or explain the occasion?

Below: Soldiers outside the main door of the Town Hall, Stanhope, during the First World War. The men were housed there temporarily while awaiting orders.

A Remembrance Day procession, passing the Midland Bank in Stanhope, *c.* 1970. The police lead the way, with Dr Donald Thompson and Mr Walter Turnbull heading the procession and Mr Burgess just behind. The fact that the First World War officially ended at the eleventh hour on the eleventh day of the eleventh month was seen as 'mystical' and a good omen by the superstitious. The reality for the post-war world was harsh, as Western Europe faced up to the economic ruin that followed and counted the cost of 2 ½ million dead and even more disabled. Remembrance Day was a way of honouring the dead, and processions such as this took place throughout the country until the Second World War and resumed in many places afterwards.

A 'Peace tea' at Westgate in 1919, formally laid out with trim vases of flowers, pleated serviettes and regimented rows of chairs.

The dale at war. A WAAF detachment at Blackheath in 1943. Petite Elsie Garthwaite sits fourth from the right. Inevitably she was called 'Titch' by her comrades. She is typical of thousands of young women who volunteered for war service and in so doing saw new places and made friendships which are still enjoyed.

The TV aerial being erected above Rookhope in 1958, bringing better TV reception to upper-dale homes. In the early days of TV there were problems of reception due to the narrowness of the dale in places.

The flower shows and leek shows of the north-east are justly famous and Weardale has leek clubs and flower clubs which run shows and competitions. But the most important competitions are at the agricultural shows, where there is wider competition and cups such as these to be won. This is Mr Ed Rayden judging chrysanthemum entries at Stanhope Show.

Waiting for a driving test and vehicle check at Cowgarth Green. The now demolished barn and vanished west gateway of the castle can be seen in the background.

Six

Hearth and Home and Family

A photograph taken at Widley Field to commemorate the wedding anniversary of Mr George Garthwaite and his wife Mary. The group includes their children, Jonathan, Lizzie, Jack, Nellie and Jack, who are standing behind them. The photograph was taken by Frank Emerson who, in addition to his studio in Paragon Street, travelled around the dale taking groups such as this one on home ground.

Above: A Wolsingham Grammar School group class of 1933. The master is Mr Witton. On the right hand end of the front row is Elsie Garthwaite who, as Mrs Elsie Allison, is a well-known member of the Stanhope community. Other members in the group are, back row, left to right: Annie Walton, Deborah ?, Nancy Goodwin, Bessie Hood, Lily Sleightholm, Connie Brown. Front row: Vera Lonsdale, Isabel Dagg, Jean Bell, Marjorie Kidd, Gladys ?.

Left: Could anything be more delightful than these 'three little maids' with their wide-sashed dresses and appealing expressions. They come from the Garthwaite family album. Tartan was made fashionable by Queen Victoria and Prince Albert and persisted for many years in furnishings and dress as in the girls' sashes. The two bigger girls are Annie and Bella Hunter.

Above: A Garthwaite family wedding at Westgate, *c.* 1913. Mr Jack Garthwaite sits beside his bride, Miss Frances Hetherington. Behind the groom is Mr Tom Garthwaite and his future wife, and behind the bride is Mr and Mrs Lomax. The bride's elegant dress, adorned with a corsage (no bouquet), would have been described as 'an afternoon gown' in Edwardian magazines.

Right: The burns in the dale—Middlehope, Stanhope and Wasterley—are popular places for walking. This informal photograph of young Tom Garthwaite in his Sunday best was taken during an afternoon stroll in Stanhope Dene and uses the Dene as a backcloth.

Above: A school group from the Council School, Stanhope, *c.* 1932. There was a healthy rivalry between this school and the Anglicans of the Barrington. Scuffles on the way home were common and snow afforded good opportunities to settle scores. The children from this school would line up snowballs on the high wall ready to pelt the C of Es from their vantage point as they passed by. But the Barrington boys would also be prepared; they would tell the girls to run past quickly while they distracted the Council School children with their own 'ammunition'.

Left: A marriage uniting two well-known family names: the Stephenson–Walton wedding of around 1910. Descendants of both families still live in the dale.

Above: Getting to the church on time. Everyone knows how important weddings are, everyone wishes to give the young couple a good 'send off', and they are a wonderful opportunity for a family get together. So when the rigours of the 1947 winter prevented the Millicans of Backstone, near Wolsingham, from using their car, they resorted to a sledge rather than miss such a special occasion. The sledge was presumably horse-drawn.

Right: A mother, Mrs Hewitson, and her three daughters, *c.* 1919. Hewitsons were farming at Old Park and Horsleyburn around this time.

Members of the Ridley family: a pretty mother and two boys. The younger is still in dresses while the older boy has been 'breeched'. The leopard skin must have been one of the photographer's 'props'—one wonders if the children were frightened. Many parents would object to its use in this environmentally conscious age.

Phoebe Ridley on the garden path leading to the seventeenth-century door of Peakfield farmhouse, c. 1919. She was just about to be taken to one of the many fancy dress parties held in the interwar years.

Above: Boys brought up on farms usually show an early interest in the farm. This boy, dressed in a replica of his father's outfit—thick breeches, waistcoat, jacket, and a flat cap, has evidently taken to the farming life and has both a lamb and a goat beside him for his photograph. Goat's milk is sometimes used to feed orphan lambs.

Right: Private Joseph (Jossie) Pattinson, his wife Maude Amanda, and their tiny daughter Annie, c. 1917. Private Pattinson was one of many who volunteered for active service from the dale—a response echoed throughout the country. He was one of the lucky ones in that he came home; the war memorial outside the churchyard and the plaque inside St Thomas' list those who did not. During the war Joseph Pattinson's company was sent to Stanhope while awaiting orders. Although he and others were local men they were not allowed home, but had to sleep in 'emergency quarters' in the Town Hall.

Walter Turnbull, dressed in his best suit with his hair carefully parted down the middle, stands posed in the photographer's studio to be recorded for posterity.

Walter Turnbull, now grown up, stands behind his mates Tommy Gowland and Joseph (Joe) Sanderson, not in a studio this time but out in the Dene.

Right: Lynda Turnbull, daughter of the little girl who sat on her mother's knee beside her soldier dad, is seen here feeding a lamb at her aunt and uncle's farm at Bridge End, Frosterley, around 1960. She herself is now married and a mother.

Below: The workshop at Stanhope Mill when Mr Philipson lived there. Maggie Turnbull in her white pinny stands in front of her father, Walter, who lived at Stanhope Mill. The other man in an apron is Joseph (Joe) Wearmouth, who later married Ella Parker. Today Ella Wearmouth is 93 years young and looking forward to a centenary party even better than the memorable one she gave for her 90th.

Left: Pedal power. The advent of the bicycle increased people's mobility and gave them a freedom to explore. It also had some effect on ladies' fashions. This slightly flared long skirt, with trim blouse and tie and a hat that will stay on (provided it is secured with hat pins) was regarded as a suitable outfit for the biker.

Below: A photograph of the Bee family of St John's Chapel given to Beamish Museum some years ago. The identification suggested is that Mr Fred Bee and Mrs Bee (Westgate born) are seated with their family around them, one of whom is Robert who at the age of 16 won the £100 prize for the 110 yards handicap at the Morpeth races, although five years earlier he had been badly injured and had been on crutches for about a year. He was killed in the First World War.

Right: A very 'Victorian' group with its backcloth of trailing ivy: Mr John Holroyd with Mrs Humble behind and Jane Ann Ridley kneeling beside him. The lady on the left is not known.

Below: The Pickerings of Newlandside waiting to have afternoon tea in the garden. Mrs Raine is sitting in the folding chair at the left.

A sombre photograph of a family mourning group.

Three ladies enjoying the sun and a chat outside Unthank Hall, Stanhope. Their pleasant dignified features suggest that they are members of the same family; two ladies have been identified as Mrs Gardiner (left) and her mother (centre).

Right: A walk to Tumbling Bridge, a pleasant way to spend a Sunday afternoon.

Below: A group of children from Westgate School out with their teacher. The dale is a wonderful teaching resource and it is clear that these children are enjoying their outing.

The photographs above and below are included for two reasons: to make a point about the need to identify the subject matter of any photograph, and to illustrate the detail of interesting costume. How much more valuable they would be if we only knew who they were. The crinoline lady below could be as early as 1865, the other one around 1890.

Mr Ralph Rutherford of Copt Hill and his wife Mary Anne, née Walton. They farmed at Copt Hill, an interesting old farmhouse at the head of the dale, for many years. The farm is now kept by Mr and Mrs George Robinson, helped by their young son Thomas. As a sign of the times, 'B&B' has been added to the farm's activities.

Liza Shuttle had her photograph taken the very day she received her new bicycle in 1920. Mr Starkey's invention of the 'safety cycling machine' in 1885 was a tremendous boon as it gave to thousands of people a freedom of movement hitherto only enjoyed by the more affluent. Its invention came at a time when girls were being allowed a little more freedom, so that they, as well as the men, were able to take advantage of the push-pedal bike.

The Waltons of Westgate: a family group at Crag Villa, *c.* 1912. There have been Waltons in Weardale since at least the late sixteenth century. Back row, left to right: Mary Walton who married Tom Coulthard, John Willy who worked for Bainbridge's shop in Newcastle (who themselves came from the dale), Emmaline (so-called because she was born when the railway came up the dale!), and Maggie who also married a Coutlhard, Joe who worked on the railway, and Jenny who left the dale. Front row: Anne who became a schoolteacher at Eastgate and rode to school on her motor bike, Mr Thomas Walton, a stonemason and stick dresser, Thomas Eric, Frank Walton's father, kneels in the middle. At the right is Arthur Walton who worked as a clerk at Eastgate station.

Vicar Pattison gave Mr Robert (Bobby) Reed's grandfather some glass plate photographs, one of which was this treasure of a photograph of him and his family at the door of Glebe Cottage, St John's Chapel, *c.* 1912. Joseph is smoking his long churchwarden's pipe while young Joseph plays the melodion. Mary Ann (b. 1905), who is to be Mr Reed's mother, sits on the stool beside him. Phoebe and Robert sit at the other side. All the children are wearing serviceable clogs. Sadly Robert died when only 17, Joseph by the time he was 23, both victims of the scourge of the age—TB. The clarity of the photograph and the grace of the composition is remarkable. James Whitehead Pattison, vicar of St John's Chapel 1906-1930, left a cache of similar photographs recording life in Weardale. When his daughter died most went to Bowes Museum, but some, like this one, are still in the dale. Glebe Cottage and its whinstone cobbles (from Copt Hill) still nestles down the lane beside the Town Hall that leads to the showfield.

Class III, Wearhead Council School, *c.* 1910. Names are unknown but there is much to be seen in looking at the clothes. Children in these earlier photographs often look so very solemn, but cameras were not so fast then and they had to stay quite still until the photographer gave the all clear.

Miss Nellie Dawson (at the back, left) and Miss Barbara Backhouse, with their pupils at Wearhead School, *c.* 1950.

Teachers Herbert Slack and Mary Temperley stand with their pupils for the annual school photo session—and Mr C. Cridge knows all their names. Back row, left to right: Tom Nicholson, Alb Slack, Joe Nattress, T. Indian, Alf Maddison, Jack Pattison, R. Wilkinson, Joe Bowman, Wilf Gray. Middle row: Roy Heatherington, G. Thompson, J. Sanderson, R. Ripley, Ken Ridley, H. Wearmouth, J. Ridley, Norman Swatten, Stan Wilkinson, Reg Spark, Geoffrey Slack. Front row: Vera Armstrong, Jean Hodgson, Amy Lonsdale, Ella Bibby, Doris Walton, Adelaide Angus, Jenny Woodhall, Bessie Bee, Jenny Coulthard, Tom Potts, Danny Bibby. Where are they now, this class of 1930? The late Mr Reg Spark became manager of the Co-op.

John Bee, on a happy day out with the family, was run over and killed by Lord Londonderry's coach, c. 1935. This portrait is in so many homes in the dale, it would seem to be a commemorative photograph of a young life cut short.

Margaret Currah, holding a favourite doll, poses for her photograph on what appears to be a rather uncomfortable spindly bench, c. 1932. From the Parson Byers farming family, she became Mrs Wilkinson later in life and is well known in the village for her involvement in church activities and fund-raising for Red Cross, Children in Need and other charities.

A picture of a carefree childhood, c. 1914. The little girl wears the type of sunbonnet used by daleswomen when hay-making and she is obviously enjoying being pulled along by her brother in the iron-wheeled dog cart. In late Victorian and Edwardian times well-to-do families often had dogs (usually St Bernards) to pull such carts along.

There was considerable excitement among the children of Rookhope when this vixen cub was captured, and they pose proudly for their photograph. Their enthusiasm is not shared by the fox; her baleful and wary look suggests she is only biding her time to try and escape.

Three Sisters of Mercy with their charges in the gardens of St Anne's Convent School, founded in 1892. This photograph was probably taken about 1910 and shows all the school. It has not been possible to identify the individuals. The school plays its part in the community; only this year pupils have contributed to the Wolsingham Parish Map which is to hang in the Town Hall.

Sister Cecilia of St Anne's sent this photographic postcard to Front Street, Wolsingham, in 1934. Evidently there were examinations in the air for the card was to tell Miss Thelma Dowson that she was 'quite safe—she had 86 this time; Mavis was top with 96 and there was only one below 80'. The picture shows parts of the school not usually seen by passers-by: the school tennis court and garden, the back of the school building, and the chapel.

Children of the Stanhope Wesleyan School, Back Lane, Stanhope, which opened in 1877. It became the Stanhope Board School in 1894 and by the time this photograph was taken in around 1910 it was Stanhope Council School. The building is now part of the Methodist church and is used for church events. The children are gathered to admire a map of Europe made in sand in the playground. Behind them Ashes Quarry is still busily working.

A farmer's wife in the making? A young competitor shows her ducks at Weardale Show in 1936, probably at St John's Chapel.

The shield winners of Crawleyside School, 1910-13. A treasured photograph from Mr and Mrs C. Cridge's collection. There are still pines growing at the spot where this photograph was taken, but the village school, like the chapel of ease, has long gone. They were built to serve the needs of the community when quarrying and mining were still providing work for local men. As those industries declined so did the population. Although taken eighty years ago, some of the children can be identified. In the centre of the back row are Jos Elliot and Jack. Second from left in the third row is Bessie Thirlwell, fourth is Dora Harrison, sixth is Ishbel Elliot, eighth is Maggie Forster, ninth is Eva Lonsdale. Fourth from left in the second row is Sydney Harrison, fifth is Wilf Elliot, sixth is M. Thirlwell (father of the just retired headmaster of Barrington School, Stanhope), eleventh is Lizzie Middleton. Third from left in the front row is Isaac Brown, sixth is Mary Harrison, tenth is Magnus Egglestone.

Lintzgarth on the Rookhope Burn, c. 1915. The Lintzgarth Farm was a stock farm carved from the High Forest around 1300; its name then was Fallowhirst. It is still a small farm. Mr and Mrs Adamson stand at the gate with two of their three daughters. The little one is probably Olive.

Mr and Mrs Tom Coulthard standing proudly outside Rennie Close, their home on the 'back road', Westgate. Stone is the traditional building material of the dale, including stone slab roofs. Here the traditional walling material has been used, but the 'polite' style of architecture has been superimposed upon the vernacular. The roof is slate and has fancy ridge tiles; the stone is regularly cut, with mortar neatly patterned; hoop-style railings often seen in public parks complete the picture.

Westerhopeburn on the 'back road' near Eastgate, a most attractive seventeenth-century group of long low buildings with mullioned windows and stone slab roof. Westerhopeburn was one of the ten new farms founded by the bishops' officers (1410–1419) and placed on the boundary of Stanhope Park, the upkeep of whose boundary wall was the responsibility of the then farmers. However, the area had evidently already been used for summer grazing of stock as its old name was Westanburn*shele*.

The remains of Old Woodcroft on the 'back road' between Stanhope and Frosterley. Woodcroft Hall is marked on the earliest map of County Durham. The ruin has deteriorated still further since this photograph was taken, but the remains of a gin gan (the polygonal wheelhouse containing the horse-powered horizontal wheel used for threshing) and a wall dovecot are visible, and there is a hint of a medieval building on the site. Fortunately it has been surveyed by the North East Vernacular Architecture Group.

A parlour at Rookhope at the turn of the century. No easy chairs here to permit any relaxation, but upright chairs to keep the back straight.

Bradley Hall, Wolsingham, as it was until the early nineteenth century. A 'clod of a steward' (from Dr Devey's *Records of Walsingham*, 1926) took most of this southern face of the old part of the house down in order to repair walls and build farm buildings. All that remains now are the three arched, vaulted chambers of the ground floor and some odd bits. The 'modern' house, built about 1820, is behind this block and at right angles to it. This southern façade was probably erected by the Bowes family, who received it in 1569 as a reward for their loyalty in the Rising of the North, after the Bradley estate had been forfeited to the Crown because of the Tempests' involvement in the rebellion.

Left: Not a home but 'The House', that is the Workhouse which so many dreaded in the nineteenth century and during the inter-war depression. During the Second World War the Workhouse was used as an emergency hospital for people evacuated from Tyneside, where bombing was a threat. In 1950 it was considerably refurbished, named Weardale House and used as a residential home. This photograph shows the laundry just before it was altered into a private residential care home. The main building now stands forlorn and empty.

Below: The trim little villa built for the manager of Rookhope mines, replacing the old Bug and Fly farmhouse which was on the same site, *c.* 1914.

Thomas Currah standing outside his home at West End, Stanhope.

In the days before good flashlights and fast-speed cameras, interior shots were difficult for the non-professional photographer, so interior views are relatively rare. This is one of the drawing room at Mayfield at the very end of the last century.

Above: A leisurely tea in the garden—a real period piece. The basket chair and wooden rocker, the pattern fringed cloth, the wasp waistlines, full skirts and high necks with complicated collars all add up to a clear impression of 'men and manners' at the time.

Left: William Marsden, his wife and their children outside their home.

The gardens of Newton House, Stanhope, with lovely lead statues and a lily pond in the garden, c. 1935. By this time it was in fact an hotel.

What a contrast with the affluent, genteel Newtown is this photograph of Crooks Aller at the top of the dale, built in true Weardale vernacular without a hint of outside influence.

Cragside Farm, Eastgate—Estyatshele. An old grandfather clock and armchair stand in a room with seventeenth-century panelling and an eight-panel door; a rare interior photograph indeed from the Ward family album. It was in this kitchen that the first Methodists of Eastgate had their meetings and decided to form a society. Cragside was the home of the Bainbridge family for about seventy years, until 1858. It was the birthplace of Emerson Muschamp Bainbridge (1817–92) who, in 1847, founded the famous shop in Newcastle-upon-Tyne which was said to be the first department store in Europe.

Seven

Village Elders

Many places in the dale are associated with men and women who have left their mark on the area; some dramatically, as at Attwood's Steelworks, some more modestly, like the daffodils at Shull. It is pleasant when wandering about the dale to be reminded of those who have contributed to the local environment or community. It is interesting, too, to see photographs of such village elders and try to fathom what they were really like. This portrait of John Roddam of Newtown hints at the kindness of the man who helped the families of striking quarry workers in 1892 and contributed to many charities.

John Lee of the Limes, Westgate, seen here playing with a young Frank Walton, c. 1940. John Lee loved his Weardale, was a committed Methodist and an enthusiastic student of the dale of his father's and grandfather's time. His writings preserved old stories and personalities for posterity, many of them centred upon Westgate. As H.L. Honeyman wrote in the Foreword to Weardale Memories and Traditions, he had 'praiseworthy sympathy for the underdogs' which led to his being outspoken about absentee rectors, absentee landlords, mainly the Ecclesiastical Commissioners, and absentee employers—mainly the min, owners. It was to Frank Walton that John Lee gave the very first copy of his now rare book.

William Morley Egglestone (1838-1921): journalist, botanist, historian, archivist, geologist, sanitary inspector, secretary to the Stanhope Band, the cricket club and many other organizations. 'Old Penny a liner', as he was sometimes affectionately called, wrote many pamphlets on the history, geology, flora and fauna and legends of the dale. He made a significant contribution to heightening people's awareness of the beauty and heritage of Weardale. His 1891 pamphlet, urging the extension of the railway from Stanhope to Wearhead, was influential in its day, and today is so useful in giving a view of the dale in the closing years of the last century that it has recently been republished by the Weardale Museum.

Dr Gray presenting the Gray Cup at the former Barrington School, High Street. Included in the photograph are Mr Ray, headmaster (with watch chain), and on his right Mrs Gray of Ury House (now Glenroy), Stanhope. The medical practitioners of the dale have made a tremendous contribution, well beyond the call of duty, to the well being of the dale, as have the educators. The 'Barrington' is now three houses; this group is outside the eastern end, now the home of Mr and Mrs A. Raine who have preserved the plaque recording the opening of the school in 1869. James Benson and Rebecca Lowrey were the first teachers, and the architect was Ewan Christian, designer of the National Portrait Gallery in London.

Lady Chaytor of Witton Castle with her attendants—a boy to push her three-wheeled basket chair, a lady companion, and her lap dog. The Chaytors were influential landowners on the edge of the dale, owning estates in the Witton-le-Wear area as well as around Croft, and used the dale in the shooting season. Members of the family served as Justices of the Peace and Lord and Deputy Lieutenants of the county. This picture, which was probably taken outside Mayfield, Wolsingham, was sent to the butler of Auckland Castle after Lady Chaytor had been staying there.

William Pentland of Midlothian House, a leading resident of Ireshopeburn around 1920. What a vitality and zest for life is captured here. The photographer is unknown but the work is worthy of a professional. Mr Pentland was an Anglican, a persuasion not over plentiful in the upper dale in his day. If we did not know already, the glass and bottle would inform us that Mr Pentland was no Methodist.

148

Dr William Robinson (1859–1942) was born in Croft House, Stanhope, then newly built by his father. He gained wealth and reputation during his long medical career. His early training was more akin to an apprenticeship, but he did attend Armstrong College to complete his training and later took his surgeon's qualification by post. He practised in Stanhope for many years, was medical officer to the lead companies and wrote research papers on the high local incidence of thyroid problems and on miners' lung diseases. He married Miss Eleanor Rippon of Rogerley Hall and lived at Butts House. Their son Geoffrey Stanhope married one of his Rippon cousins and changed his name to Rippon. Dr Robinson is best remembered now for the foundation of the TB sanatorium at Stanhope and for his work at Sunderland Eye Infirmary, whose centenary history he wrote. During his lifetime he was best known for having the first bathroom, complete with flushing toilet, in Stanhope. He is buried in the family plot in St Thomas' churchyard under a wartime utility tombstone.

Major George Alan Lister of Wolsingham. Many Weardalians have been interested in the history of the dale—the names of W.H. Hildyard, W.M. Egglestone, J.J. Graham and John Lee come to mind. Major Lister was one of their number; he spent many years studying the history and archaeology of the dale and assembling a collection of artefacts. In addition he was also a poet; his book Rhymes of a Weardale Lad reveal his love for the area.

Now there is a new generation in the dale continuing the tradition of poetry and study. John Anderson's *Weardale Reflections* around a Farmer's Hearth upholds the tradition of locally inspired verse. Peter Bowes' Clearing the Forest has set a new standard for successors to emulate. And here is Major Lister's son Alan carrying on his father's tradition of investigation. He has had a particular interest in the archaeology of the dale since schooldays when he first helped on a 'dig'.

The Stanhope Band playing the workers and their banner from East End down to the Co-op field. Thomas Miles Sexton, then headmaster of the County School, stands outside his home, No. 1 Dales Terrace, which was the family home from the time it was built until around 1985 when Mrs Eva Forster, the last member of the family to live there, moved to a smaller house. The house is important in the history of the local Labour party branch, which was formed around 1920 as a result of animated discussions between the Sextons and their friends, many of whom were former pupils of Tom Sexton. Mr Sexton was MP for the Barnard Castle area from 1935 until 1945.

Opposite below: The opening of Fairfield, Stanhope, as district offices of the Rural District Council, *c.* 1940. Dr Bannerman is standing at the left front with Revd John Thompson, the curate, then James Ridley and Tom Proud beside him. In the second row are Mr and Mrs Austen. At the back are Bert Ward (left) and John Best, with Amy Walton in front of him. The other men in the group are Harry Coulthard, Willie Pattinson, John Walton, and at the right Walter Turnbull.

As the 'Big House' of Stanhope, it might be expected that the castle would be a great asset to the neighbourhood, providing employment and, in hard times, relief. However, this was true only for a relatively short period between 1798 and 1855. Before Cuthbert Rippon built his fine house on Castle Heugh there was only a small cottage there. Although his son, Cuthbert Rippon MP, considerably extended both house and estate, by 1855 he was facing financial ruin. Thereafter the castle had mainly seasonal occupants—usually early autumn shooting parties—until after the Second World War. The Pease family of Darlington railway fame leased it from the Church Commissioners during the 1880s and 1890s, Richard Cooper Powell was the tenant around 1902, Sir Richard Ashmore Cooper in 1905 and the Bainbridge family during the 1920s. So it was up to families such as the Roddams and the Rectors, who were on hand in the late nineteenth and the first half of the twentieth century, to provide help to the often needy people of the parish.

The 'monument' in the photograph is a drinking fountain erected in 1877 to the memory of John Joseph Roddam, engineer, of Newtown House. John Watson Roddam, estate and land agent, demolished old Newtown and built the new house around 1905 in the hope of improving his wife's health. At the same time he moved the drinking fountain erected to his father's memory from Cowgarth Hill to its present site and planted the trees (now fully grown) against the fence. He was a Justice of the Peace and very influential in local affairs.

Wesley's message was first preached in Weardale in 1748 by Christopher Hopper, less than 50 yards from where this chapel at Westgate was built. 'When we came into the dales', Hopper wrote, 'we met with a very cold reception ... I preached under the walls of an old castle. A few children and two or three old women attended, who looked hard upon us. When I had done we followed them into their houses and talked freely to them in their own language ... Sometime after I preached in private houses, ale houses, cockpits or wherein I could find a door open ... This was the beginning of the good work in Weardale which has continued until this very day.' This Wesleyan chapel was built in 1791 by stone masons from Hexham who then went on to build the Hare and Houds in the village. Both buildings still stand. The Hare and Hounds is still a pub, but the chapel (now holiday cottages) was closed in 1938. For a time it was a dance hall, much to the horror of a local Methodist who thought 'demolition with honour' preferable to such 'survival with dishonour'.

![Ling Riggs farmhouse]

Above: Ling Riggs, a secluded farm high on the fells of the upper-dale—not an easy area to farm yet it was in existence before 1600 along with other farms such as High Wham, Lanehill and Ullsfield. The Watsons farmed Ling Riggs for many generations. Stephen Watson provided bed and board for John Wesley on some of his visits to the dale. The last Watson to live here was the late Constance (Concie) Watson who, as Mrs Milburn, made a significant contribution to the community by founding the St John's Chapel Music Festival.

Right: Shull House (usually called St John's) was part of the estate of Backhouse the bankers. From 1847 to 1902 it was the home of first William Backhouse and then of his son Charles. Both father and son were keen daffodil fanciers and their work won national recognition. Their legacy is still enjoyed every springtime when the Weardale Perfection (Charles' greatest achievement) transforms the lawns into a carpet of golden yellow. Local tradition says that the house was used for Methodist services during the 1880s. Now a farm, it was a Youth Hostel for some years after the war.

The high and imposing 1885 Primitive Methodist chapel at Wolsingham now houses a business making four-poster beds for 'up-market' shops like Harrods, but it is still a reminder of its architect George Race. At the time it was built, 'chapel', whether PM or Wesleyan, was at the centre of many people's lives. Social events and education as well as spiritual support were offered. Wesley's teaching of personal religion, associated with his message of moderation, the work ethic and self-improvement, was of inestimable benefit to Weardale. In the nineteenth century many local Methodists made a significant contribution to the community. The Race family are a good example: George Race senior was a prominent Primitive Methodist; his Westgate home was a centre for lively discussion groups and for visiting ministers. He had a masterly understanding of Weardale geology and his pamphlet on the subject is one of the smaller treasures of the Weardale Museum. George Race junior was an inspiring preacher, builder, architect and first-class cabinet maker. Nathan Race was an eloquent spokesman for the lead miners. The Race family were living in the dale before Christopher Hopper tramped over the hills to preach near the Wapping, Westgate, in 1748, and the family is still represented in the Upper Town, Westgate.

Dryderdale Hall, on the southern edge of Wolsingham parish, is a solid late nineteenth-century mansion set in pleasant grounds. It was built by Alfred Backhouse of Pillmore Hall, Darlington, in an area known as Shull. The Backhouses were a prolific Quaker family, important in banking, railway development, prison reform, industry, natural history and agricultural improvement. When the socially prestigious book *Durham at the Opening of the Twentieth Century* was published five Backhouses were listed. Shull House is an older building on the same estate (p. 155).

The opening of the improved Stanhope Dene in 1892. The ceremony took place at the Roddam Bridge, named in honour of J.W. Roddam who had been one of the leading benefactors to the needy quarry workers' families.

Grazing cattle, haystack, water and trees all make a truly rural scene behind Holywood Hall—the symbol of Charles Attwood's (1791–1875) industrial successes at Wolsingham and Tow Law. Charles was one of the seven sons of Matthias Attwood, a Halesowen banker. Charles and his brother Thomas (1783–1856) were well-known political radicals of their day. Charles founded the Northern Political Union in Newcastle. Thomas was prominent in union affairs and an outspoken agitator for electoral reform. He had a brilliant start to his career—High Bailiff of Birmingham and a wealthy banker by the age of 28, and sat in the Reform Parliament of 1832. Charles had a more uncertain start, in glass and soap making in Newcastle, his success coming fairly late in life. Yet Charles left a flourishing business to his nephew and the Holywood Hall estate, while Thomas died relatively poor.

Above: The old houses at Huntshieldford remind us of William Morley Egglestone for it was his birthplace and home for many years, though later in life he settled in Dales Terrace, Stanhope. Huntshieldford (the local pronunciation is 'Hunshelford') is the site of an early shieling in the forest of Weardale. A hundred years ago there was a cluster of sixteen families here, but not now. The house on the right is derelict and its lovely cottage garden overgrown.

Right: Mr Walter Turnbull, Weardale born and bred, was glad to settle down again in Stanhope after the war, and to spend the rest of his working life in the employment of the Rural District Council. He was heavily involved in many local societies and in church affairs, including being leader of the Scouts, assistant secretary and vice-president of Stanhope Show, chairman of the Stanhope branch of the British Legion, secretary of the Stanhope Silver Band and church treasurer. The vitality of community life is enhanced by the contributions of people like Walter Turnbull. The dale is fortunate that now, as then, there are people like him working for the good of the community.

Acknowledgements

The generosity of friends and neighbours in lending photographs and providing information is warmly acknowledged. They all deserve to be mentioned by name: Mrs E. Allinson, L. Aberdeen, Miss B. Backhouse, Mr and Mrs Cridge, Mrs A. Dargue, Miss N. Dawson, Mrs Ripley, Mrs M. Gibbons, Mrs Dixon, Mr P. Bowes, Mr J. Cockayne, Dr J.L. Crosby, Mr D. Hutchinson, Mr A. Lister, Mr J. Mellody, Professor T.R. Milburn, Mr R. Reed, Mr J. Robinson, Mr Frank Walton, Blue Circle Cement, and particularly Mrs Ann Harrison, Mrs Ruby Ridley and Mrs Annie Turnbull who allowed me to raid both their family archives and their memories. I hope that no one has been inadvertently omitted, but if they have, then sincere apologies. All help received has been warmly appreciated. Thanks must also be given to the Photographic Archive of Beamish Museum and to Mr Bill Lawson of that department. Mr Issy Thompson with his reaper.